IMAGES
of America

HALF MOON
BAY

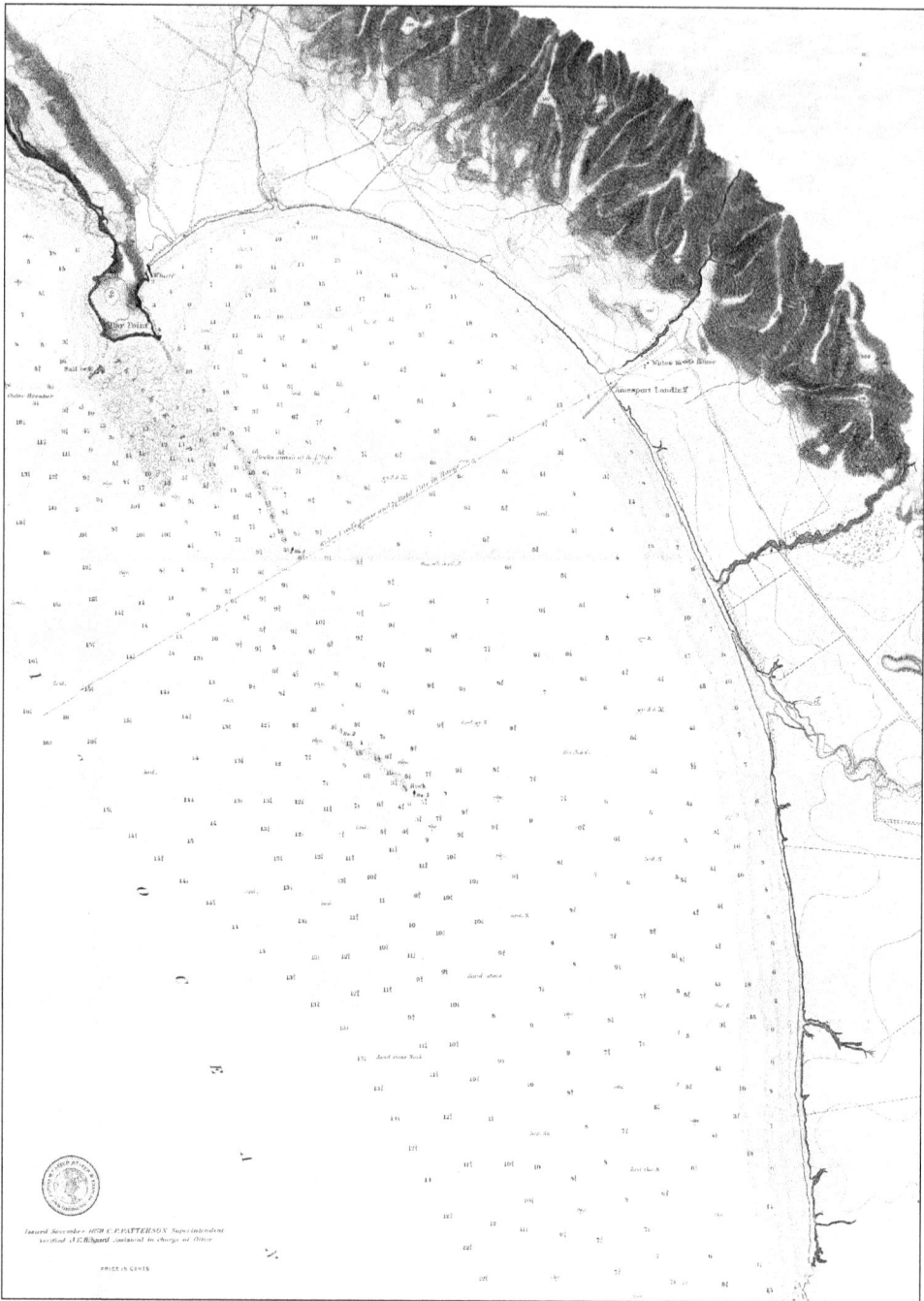

Above is an 1863 map of Half Moon Bay, California, that was originally drafted under the direction of A.D. Bache, superintendent of the Survey of the Coast of the United States, and later corrected to 1885. Important features include Pillar Point, Sail Rock, Amesport Landing, and the ocean depths.

ON THE COVER: Dated February 28, 1924, this photo shows Highway 1 by the Half Moon Bay Beach. (Courtesy of Jim Bell.)

IMAGES
of America

HALF MOON BAY

Kathleen Manning and Jerry Crow

ARCADIA
PUBLISHING

Published by Arcadia Publishing
Charleston, South Carolina

Library of Congress Catalog Card Number: 2004113947

For all general information contact Arcadia Publishing at:
Telephone 843-853-2070
Fax 843-853-0044
E-mail sales@arcadiapublishing.com
For customer service and orders:
Toll-Free 1-888-313-2665

Visit us on the Internet at www.arcadiapublishing.com

This early photo of Ocean Shore Railroad shows a passenger train coming into Montara c. 1917.

4

CONTENTS

ACKNOWLEDGMENTS

The authors appreciate the insights and access to images afforded to us by Ron Micklesen of the Half Moon Bay Nursery, Dave Cresson of the Zaballa House, Carol Micklesen and Glenn Regan of the San Benito House, and the staff of the Miramar Beach Restaurant.

We are deeply appreciative of the work, sharp eyes, and patience of Andrea Souza, who was indispensable in assembling the components of the book. Sandy Cavallaro helped us with the text and kept us laughing.

Sources of the images include Jim Bell of Mother Nature's Cupboard, Tahoe; the family of Lloyd Easterby; the Half Moon Bay Public Library; the Clyde Jenkins collection, Pacifica Historical Society; the Library of Congress—American Experience; Ron Powell; San Mateo Historical Museum exhibits; Karen Solomon; Armando and Dan Vargas, Images of the Past, Tiburon; Kathleen Manning; and Jerry Crow.

REFERENCES

Cloud, Roy W. *History of San Mateo County*. Chicago: S.J. Clarke, 1928.

Companys, F. Boneu. *Gaspár de Portolá*. Lerida, Spain: Instituto de Estudios Berdenses, 1983.

Costanso, Miguel. *Diary of the Portolá Expedition, 1769–1770*. Berkeley, CA: University of California, Berkeley, 1911.

Crespi, Fr. Juan. Diary, 1770, Kate Bancroft translation. Berkeley, CA: University of California, Berkeley.

Eldredge, Zoeth Skinner. *The Beginnings of San Francisco*. San Francisco: The California Promotion Committee, 1912.

Griffith, B.A. "The Half Moon Bay of Sixty Years Ago," *Half Moon Bay News*, May 19, 1923.

Gualtieri, Kathryn. *Half Moon Bay, the Birth of a Coastside Town*. Half Moon Bay, CA: Spanishtown Historical Society, 1988.

Guddle, Erwin G. *1000 California Place Names*. Berkeley, CA: University of California Press, 1949.

Moore and DePue. *Illustrated History of San Mateo County*. San Francisco, 1878.

Margolin, Malcolm. *The Ohlone Way*. Berkeley, CA: Heyday Books, 1978.

Morrall, June. *Half Moon Bay Memories*. El Granada, CA: Moonbeam Press, 1978.

Pourade, Richard F. *The Call to California*. San Diego, CA: Union-Tribune Publishing Company, 1968.

San Mateo County: Its History and Heritage. Redwood, CA: San Mateo County Historical Resources Advisory Board, 1983.

Stanger, Frank. *South from San Francisco*. Redwood City, CA: San Mateo County Historical Association, 1963.

Svanevik, Michael and Shirley Burgett. *The County Chronicles*. 1990.

U.S. Geological Survey, Report No. 94-4151.

Wagner, Jack. *The Last Whistle*. Berkeley, CA: Howell-North Books, 1974.

INTRODUCTION

The crescent-shaped arm of the Pacific Ocean forms the central section of the San Mateo County coast, stretching from the south side of Montara Mountain around past Montara, Moss Beach, Princeton-by-the-Sea, El Granada, Miramar, Half Moon Bay, and to the ghost of the once-bustling Purisima village near Miramontes Point.

The natural enclosure originally attracted early Spanish missionaries and settlers to raise cattle, horses, and sheep with little fear of their livestock wandering off. The first town of San Benito evolved from the intertwined lives of the Guerrero y Palomares, Vanquez, and Miramontes families who were given the three land grants and still define some aspects of the area. European, Asian, and American settlers developed the bay and its surroundings into a thriving center of lumbering, agriculture, fishing, wine making, and floriculture.

The still semi-isolated nature of the living space has brought modern home-seekers into conflict with those who would prefer to preserve as much of the rural character of the coast as possible. These transitions were facilitated in turn by expansion of the Spanish mission system, by transfer of control to the United States after the Mexican-American War, by the advent of the Ocean Shore Railroad, by military requirements in support of the Second World War effort, and by the rapid increases in population in the surrounding areas as young veterans and their families sought affordable homes near but distinct from the high-density urban areas. Blessed

Postcards became popular with tourists in the early 1900s. This c. 1910 postcard of Pillar Point from Princeton is an actual photograph. Photos such as these were a common format and are now collector's items.

by magnificent scenery and a salubrious climate, this 40-square-mile area is an unusual and altogether charming place to live and to visit.

This book is not a comprehensive history of the area, but its purpose is to accurately portray the essence of the times in the earlier phases of life in the area by republishing a varied selection of charming prints, vintage postcards, maps, and anecdotes about some of those who came before and what they did here.

This is an aerial view of the Half Moon Bay Harbor from the mid-1950s. (Courtesy of the Lloyd Easterby family.)

One

OHLONE VILLAGES TO SAN BENITO

Archaeological evidence indicates that around 500 AD, Penutian-speaking Indians moved southwest from their former homes in the Central Valley Delta region into the San Francisco and Monterey area where Hokan-speaking people were then living. The Penutian speakers came to be known as Ohlones, probably from the Miwok word for "western people." The abundance of animal and plant life in the area provided a stable and prosperous lifestyle along the coast.

Under the authority of the Bull of Pope Alexander VI, who allocated discovery rights to the "New World" between Spain and Portugal, Spain had claimed ownership of vast sections of the New World including the entire west coast of North America. Although several European sea captains sailed along the coast over the previous 200 years, fear of the rocky headlands apparently kept them from landing in the Half Moon Bay area. The situation changed when Spanish explorers, led by Gaspar de Portolá, traveled on foot and on mules along the full extent of the coast from San Diego to San Francisco Bay.

The next 80 years saw the Spanish arrival in 1769, establishment of the missions with large ranching operations in the Half Moon Bay vicinity, secularization of the missions after the 1821 Mexican Revolution, issuance of large land grants by the Mexican government, and the founding of the village of San Benito on the banks of Pilarcitos Creek.

These engraved portraits appeared in *The History of Man* (1846) and provide a European interpretation of the natives of California.

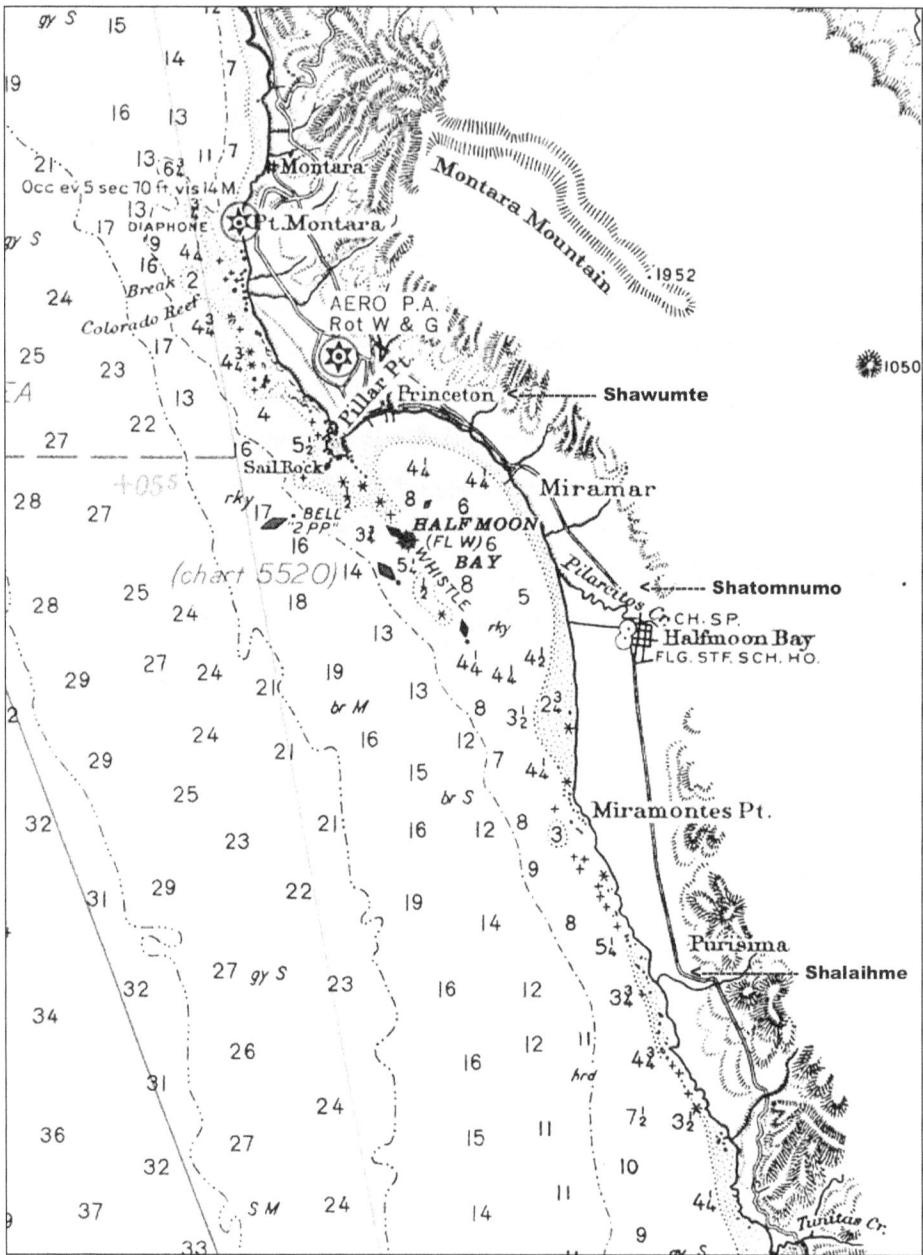

Of the estimated 1,500 Ohlones living in San Mateo County in 1770, several groups occupied villages in the Half Moon Bay area, as noted in journals of the first Europeans to arrive. Approximate village locations are indicated on this map. Shawumte (National Register of Historic Places No. 78000771) was in the vicinity of Pillar Point. The marsh at Denniston Creek would have provided game, fish, and materials commonly utilized by Ohlones, and there was a plentiful supply of clams, mussels, and abalone to be found along the shore. Shatomnumo, about 2.5 miles south of Shawumte, was probably founded back somewhat from the mouth of Pilarcitos Creek to afford some shelter from the elements. Shalaihme, on the north bank of Purisima Creek, was one of a pair of villages occupied by the clan at Purisima. The other was known as the "main camp."

At especially low tides, the tidal flats off Pillar Point are exposed for a considerable distance from shore, offering an enhanced view for nature lovers. The flats have been a source of food for the Ohlones and provided specimens for biology classes far and wide. Doc Ricketts, who figured in John Steinbeck's nonfiction book *Log from the Sea of Cortez* and his novels *Cannery Row* and *Sweet Thursday*, collected specimens here for Western Biological Laboratories.

Deer were the principal source of meat for the Ohlones, although they also ate bear, elk, rabbits, wild turkey, ducks, quail, snakes, and lizards. The hunters spent long periods in a sweat lodge to remove their scent before a hunt and utilized the head and skins of deer to disguise themselves so they could more easily get close enough for a good bow and arrow shot.

Seals, sea otters, sea elephants, and sea lions lived in large numbers along the coast prior to the 1800s. This woodcut of seals on the Farallones Islands is from the 1878 *Pacifica Coast Guide*. Spanish authorities tried to prohibit trade in seal and sea otter pelts, but demand for them was so intense that the industry grew rapidly until it had all but collapsed by the 1820s, as the animals became scarce due to over-hunting.

Naturalist Johann C.D. Schreber published *Mammals Illustrated from Nature* in 1775, including this drawing of *phoca ursine linn* as well as the next two drawings. Sea lions gather along the tidal flats along the coast between Moss Beach and Pillar Point as well as at other spots along the San Mateo County coast. The populations of elephant seals, harbor seals, and sea otters are now increasing after a severe decline.

Sea elephants were common in the area at one time, but they almost disappeared from the San Mateo County coast. In recent years, the population at Point Anno Nuevo has flourished, and there have been signs of another colony being established somewhat further north. Schreber's image is labeled *"phoca leonine linn."*

Schreber made this image of *phoca hispida*, a ringed seal common to the Arctic. This and the previous two images were engraved on copper. Harbor seals frequent spots on the local coast. The image illustrates the relatively short and inflexible front and rear flippers distinguishing seals from seal lions.

The Ohlones in this area made huts of tules tied over willow branch frames, as shown in this photo from an exhibit at the San Mateo County Historical Museum in Redwood City. The Ohlones expertly worked with wood, reeds, roots, animal skins, shells, stone, and obsidian (volcanic glass obtained by trading abalone shells and other local items with inland tribes).

Artistic license influenced some early renderings of the inhabitants. The costumes depicted in this early drawing by Hildebrand are more representative of eastern tribes than of the coastal people. Ohlones used willows and tules to build living huts, sweat lodges, grain storage bins, and boats. The sweat lodges were low-roofed structures where heat from a fire raised the air temperature to induce vigorous perspiration. Time in a sweat lodge was generally healthful and also reduced the body scent of hunters before the hunt.

14

Ohlones were highly skilled makers of baskets, which ranged in size from very small for personal items to large seed-gathering types. This illustration shows women harvesting seeds. One basket was designed to catch the falling seeds when grasses were hit with the basket edge, and another basket was designed as a backpack to carry the collected seeds. The baskets were so expertly woven that water could be kept and even boiled in them. Fire-heated rocks dropped into baskets of liquid foods such as acorn mush served to cook the contents.

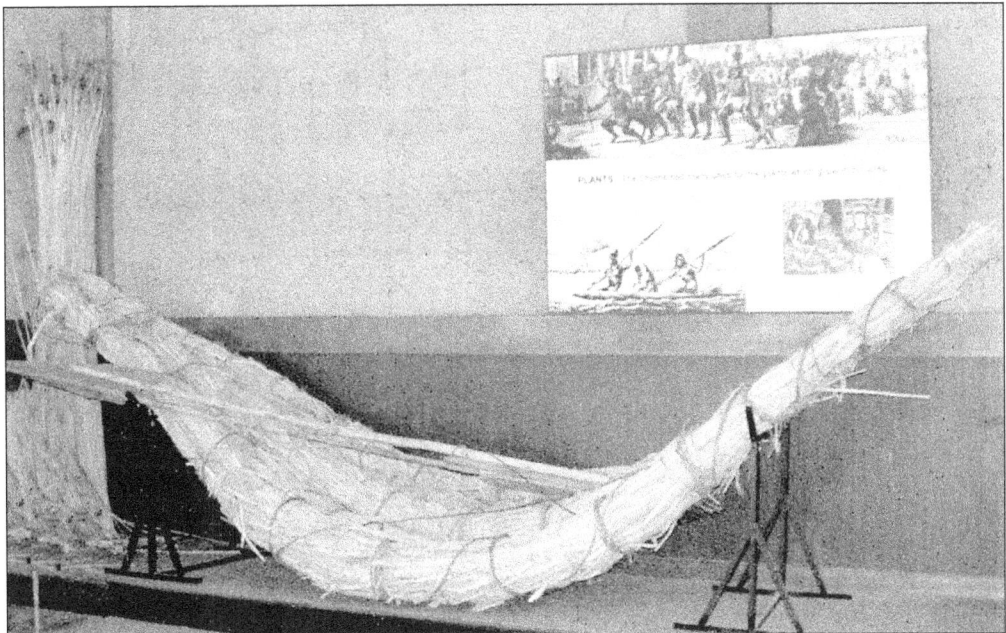

Ohlones built light, four-man boats out of tules tied with willow. Using double-bladed paddles, they could move the four-man version faster than a long boat could be rowed, according to early Spanish explorers. Despite the frail-looking nature of these craft, Ohlones were observed paddling them some distance out from shore. Pictured is a tule boat that can be found at the San Mateo County Historical Museum. The vessel is dried out but a fine example of the materials and techniques of the Ohlones.

15

In late October, 1769, Gaspar de Portolá arrived in the area with his party of soldiers, engineers, and friars. Portolá was originally sent as a lieutenant from Spain to Mexico to assist in turning the missions over to the Franciscans because the Jesuits had lost the confidence of King Carlos III of Spain. Portolá performed the sensitive task so well that he was named governor of Alta and Baja California (Alta California being roughly what is now the state of California) and was asked to lead an expedition to locate a new mission at Monterey Bay. Establishment of the mission would tangibly support the Spanish claims to ownership of lands north of Baja California and hopefully limit further southern movement of Russian hunters of seals and sea otters who were then active as far south as the Farallone Islands. Portolá failed to identify Monterey in October and returned dejected to San Diego. There he obtained additional accurate information from a sea captain and returned to complete his task at Monterey on May 23, 1770.

Portolá was born near the town of Balaguer, Spain, and is still honored there by the organization *Amics de Portolá*. Far from there, his arduous task would take him nearly 2,000 miles over often difficult terrain. Many of the men suffered from scurvy due to a lack of fruit and vegetables on the trip, but no lives were lost—a remarkable achievement for those times.

The explorers failed to recognize Monterey Bay due to inaccurate instructions. Thinking their goal was farther to the north, they pushed onward. Arriving at Purisima Creek on October 27, 1769, they found the temporarily vacant Ohlone village of Shalaihme on the north side of Purisima Creek and moved on down toward the beach to set up camp. California Landmark No. 22 commemorates the campsite, even though no physical marker exists.

The day after they arrived, the explorers camped near the mouth of Pilarcitos Creek. They had seen no trees along the way since two days prior. To the northwest they saw a bluff with two large pointed rocks offshore—Pillar Point. Many, including Portolá, were weak from dysentery, so they rested an extra day before moving on to Martini Creek north of Montara. The Pilarcitos campsite, unmarked, is California Historical Landmark No. 21.

Attempts to colonize Alta California with citizen volunteers from Spain and Mexico failed due to the hardships involved. King Carlos III then ordered the mission system expanded into largely self-sufficient settlements utilizing the Indians as the primary source of manpower. About 20 "artisan instructors" were sent from Mexico on four- to five-year contracts in 1790 to teach the Indians modern skills.

The missions controlled the area around Half Moon Bay during the late 1700s and early 1800s. The steep hills characteristic of the central county coast formed a natural enclosure or "corral de tierra," making the area suitable for keeping the cattle and horses of Mission Dolores. They grazed cattle on the grasslands north of Pilarcitos Creek and horses south of the creek.

Prior to the arrival of the Spanish, the ferocious grizzly bears so prevalent along the coastside were the primary cause of premature death among the Ohlones. To stem grizzly depredations on their cattle and horse herds, Spanish *vaqueros* hunted down the great bears on horseback with rifle and *riata* (lasso).

Spain awarded about 20 land grants during their administration of Alta California and the Mexican authorities awarded over 500. Some grants were made in lieu of salaries owed, as cash became scarce in Alta California after Mexico obtained independence from Spain in 1821. Missionaries opposed the land grants, preferring the Spanish plan of devoting half the land to support the missions and returning the other half to the Indians once they had been trained. This led to an 1827 Mexican law to expel all Spanish-born missionaries, and the division of land among those favored by the Mexican administrators continued. Tensions in San Francisco between Californios and Americans grew during the period leading up to the Mexican-American War. Guerrero, Vasquez, and Miramontes decided to move their families to the ranchos on their land grants. This section of the 1878 official San Mateo County map shows the three land grants that covered the coastside from Martini Creek to Canada Verde.

20

RANCHE—UPPER CALIFORNIA.

On October 16, 1839, Gov. Manuel Jimeno granted the northern 7,766 acres of Rancho Corral de Tierra to Francisco Guerrero y Palomares, who was the *alcalde* (mayor and magistrate) of San Francisco in 1836, 1839–1841, and 1849. The land enclosure is now Montara, Moss Beach, Princeton, El Granada, and extensive open space. Guerrero, who set up a cattle operation on the land, is believed to have built an adobe in the vicinity of Princeton in 1839.

Guerrero married Josefa de Haro, daughter of Francisco de Haro, alcalde of San Francisco, in 1838–1839. Guerrero was murdered in San Francisco in 1851, apparently over his testimony against fraudulent land claims. San Francisco's Guerrero Street was named for him because he had been well regarded by both Americans and Californios. His widow married American James Denniston. They continued to develop the holdings and gave Denniston Creek its name.

21

On October 5, 1839, Gov. Manuel Jimeno granted Tiburcio Vasquez (a member of the Anza Expedition, a soldier, and a majordomo of Mission Dolores) the southern 4,436 acres of Rancho Corral de Tierra. It covered the area from the south side of Arroyo de en Medio to the north side of Pilarcitos Creek. The family moved to the area in 1846 and built an adobe in 1848 on the north bank of Pilarcitos Creek, perhaps similar to the one in this print.

Mission Dolores priests established Pilarcitos Cemetery in 1820. It was later part of the Vasquez grant and became the burial ground for the village of San Benito. The original chapel, Our Lady of the Pillar, was built there and is commemorated by this plaque in the northwest corner. Vasquez was murdered in 1863 in a coastside saloon; both he and Guerrero had been witnesses in a famous land fraud case. His widow, Alvira Hernandez, raised their 10 children alone.

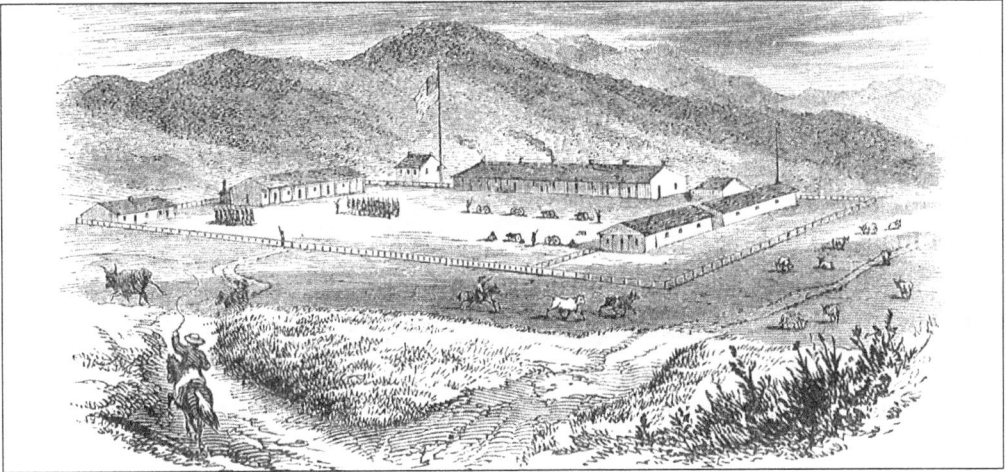

Candalrio Miramontes had been a military officer and planted Irish potatoes and a brush fence in what is now Portsmouth Square in San Francisco while residing at the Presidio with his family. He received Rancho Arroyo de los Pilarcitos (also called Rancho Miramontes), the 4,424-acre grant running from the south side of Pilarcitos Creek to the north side of Canada Verde. He built an adobe there in 1848.

Miramontes moved his large family (he had 13 children) to the rancho that soon became known as San Benito in honor of Saint Benedict, founder of the Benedictine Order. The grant boundaries now include southern Half Moon Bay: the old Spanishtown section, Arleta Park, Wavecrest, and Ocean Colony. This photograph hangs in the San Benito House.

Business was booming, but cash was scarce in Alta California after the Mexican Revolution. A money substitute was urgently needed; cattle hides and tallow filled that need. Cowhides even became known as "California banknotes." In a typical year in the late 1800s, up to 80,000 hides would be produced. The value of a cowhide averaged about $2. Boston agents purchased about 80 percent of the hides for the shoe industry.

Vasquez and Miramontes hired a contractor to build seven adobes using Tulare Indians from the central valley of California. These adobes formed the nucleus of the village that became known as San Benito, after the name Miramontes had given his rancho. Calle Real (Royal Street) ran where Main Street is today, Calle Molino became Mill Street, and Camino del Condado (County Road) headed south from where Kelly Avenue and Purisima Street cross. The village occupied roughly the area encircled on this Lloyd Easterby photograph.

Two

SAN BENITO TO SPANISH TOWN

During the Spanish and Mexican eras, agriculture was not the primary interest. The population was small and the ranchos were mainly devoted to raising cattle. Mountain ranges prevented easy access to the area. Roads were difficult to create. They were hard to repair and expensive to maintain as they wound through canyons and over mountaintops. After the huge population growth in San Francisco after the Gold Rush and California's entry into the United States, there was an enormous demand for lumber that was partly met by coastal San Mateo County. Compared to the sandy soils of San Francisco itself, the highly fertile plains and the waters from Pilarcitos Creek were enticing for early settlers who brought domesticated cattle and began serious land cultivation. Getting products to market presented a challenge to the farmers and ranchers. Toll roads, stage routes, highways, and water routes were all created to shorten the time to ship to San Francisco markets. These opportunities brought more residents to the coast. New crops and ideas resulted in an interesting blend of old and new cultures as the diverse ethnic settlers descended on the coast. To meet the needs of the new population, many businesses were created to supply the burgeoning farming, lumbering, and ranching businesses. In 1856, San Mateo County was split off from San Francisco County, resulting in more honest and responsive local government. San Benito was one of three original townships in the county. Many of the new settlers began using the name Spanishtown because Spanish was the primary language spoken then.

A c. 1898 look at Kelly Avenue shows a quiet thouroughfare, typical of small farming communities. Looking west from Main Street, a restaurant and the Occidental Hotel with its hitching post are on the left. Opposite are a horse and buggy.

The 1849 Gold Rush brought many new people to California. After seeking gold for a while, James Johnston, a Scot, got into San Francisco real estate and married Petra Maria de Haro in 1852. He bought 1,162 acres in the south section of the Miramontes grant for a ranch. He and his brother Thomas bought 800 head of cattle and drove them overland from Ohio to the new ranch. In 1853, James built this New England saltbox–style house (above) of hand-hewn redwood.

In 1861, Petra died. James returned to San Francisco and Petra's mother, Ursula, or "Melita," stayed on to raise James's three sons. James visited and continued to support the household. By 1877 James had suffered business reverses and had to surrender a part of the acreage to avoid foreclosure on his mortgage. He died in 1879 and was buried in the family cemetery plot marked by this monument.

James's son John F. Johnston inherited the house and put it back into good condition. The original interior wall coverings of cardboard were replaced with tongue-and-groove boards after wire nails became available around 1880. The interior of the house was beautifully decorated and furnished in its prime. A prominent local landmark, it became known as the "white house." It was neglected over the years and ended up in the sorry condition shown above.

The house became neglected in the 1900s and by 1972 it was a badly weathered shell. But help was on the way. The Spanishtown Historical Society and the City of Half Moon Bay began an effort to restore the house as a unique example of the architectural accomplishments of early settlers and as a museum of period artifacts. The Johnston House Foundation was established to carry on the project.

This monument marks the entrance to what will be a cluster of historic buildings at the site of the James Johnston House. The former Kelly Avenue Ocean Shore Railroad station was moved nearby and is in use for childcare. The plaque was placed during the bicentennial year of 1976. The house itself is No. 73000446 in the National Register of Historic Places.

Now restored and painted white, the James Johnston "white house" rests elegantly on the knoll a few hundred yards east of the intersection of Higgins Road and Highway 1. The interior has also been restored and the home is open to the public on a limited schedule.

In 1865, the California legislature granted a franchise to build a toll road from San Mateo to Half Moon Bay in order to improve a previous livestock road. It was financed through bonds. The cost of construction was not to exceed $20,000. It did not turn out to be a profitable venture and was deeded to the county in 1881 for $7,500.

In San Mateo, the stage—which carried passengers, mail, and a Wells Fargo strongbox—met the train from San Francisco. A team of four horses carried the passengers on a $2\frac{1}{4}$-hour trip to Spanishtown, including a harrowing ride down cliffs and switchbacks of the western slope of the mountains. The stage discharged the passengers at the Occidental Hotel at Kelly and Purisima. Stagecoach operations ceased in 1913, due in part to the popularity of the automobile.

In this photo the stage is getting ready to leave the Occidental Hotel located in Half Moon Bay at the corner of Kelly and Purisima Streets. Built in 1860, the structure lasted as a hotel until 1894 when it was destroyed by fire. It was rebuilt but later demolished after World War II, leaving only the annex that still stands at 415 Purisima.

This beautifully restored coach is part of the permanent display at the San Mateo County History Museum. It was a type used by private individuals. A sturdier version of this design was often the vehicle of choice by operators of the early stagecoach lines in the area.

San Mateo County enjoyed a redwood timber boom in the mid-1800s. Redwoods filled the eastward part of Purisima Canyon, but the terrain was so steep that operations were initially limited to making shingles that could be toted over the ridge to San Mateo on mules. Later, Borden and Hatch built a sawmill on Purisima Creek incorporating a waterpower mill previously built by Doolittle and Crumpecher in 1854. This 1889 lithograph depicts the operation. Improved roads and increasing coastside demand for lumber later attracted the interest of Danish lumber mogul Charles Hanson, who added substantial Purisima acreage to his holdings. The redwoods were nearly depleted by the 1890s. The remains of that redwood stand can be seen in Purisima Creek Redwoods Open Space Reserve. A total of 2,633 acres have been set aside by a gift from Save the Redwoods League. This delightful park is accessible via Skyline and also from the Higgins-Purisima Road.

VIEW OF RANCH (LOOKING WEST)

TOWN OF PURISSI
RESIDENCE, RANCH & PROP

Originally, many thought that Purisima (four miles south of Spanishtown, just East of Verde Road and Highway 1) would develop into the most important town on the central San Mateo Coast. It was the location of the first school and first church. This 1878 lithograph shows the farming operation of Mr. Henry Dobbel, including the store, harness, blacksmith shop, and the

A. SAN MATEO, CAL.
TY OF HENRY DOBBEL ESQ.

hotel of Richard Dogherty. That year Henry Dobbel produced 700 acres of potatoes. *McKenney's Pacific Coast Directory of 1880–1881* listed Richard Doherty [*sic*] as postmaster and saloonkeeper, F. Lanmle as blacksmith, and Rhode & Co. as general merchandise. Purisima (sometimes spelled "Purissima") was later eclipsed by Spanishtown.

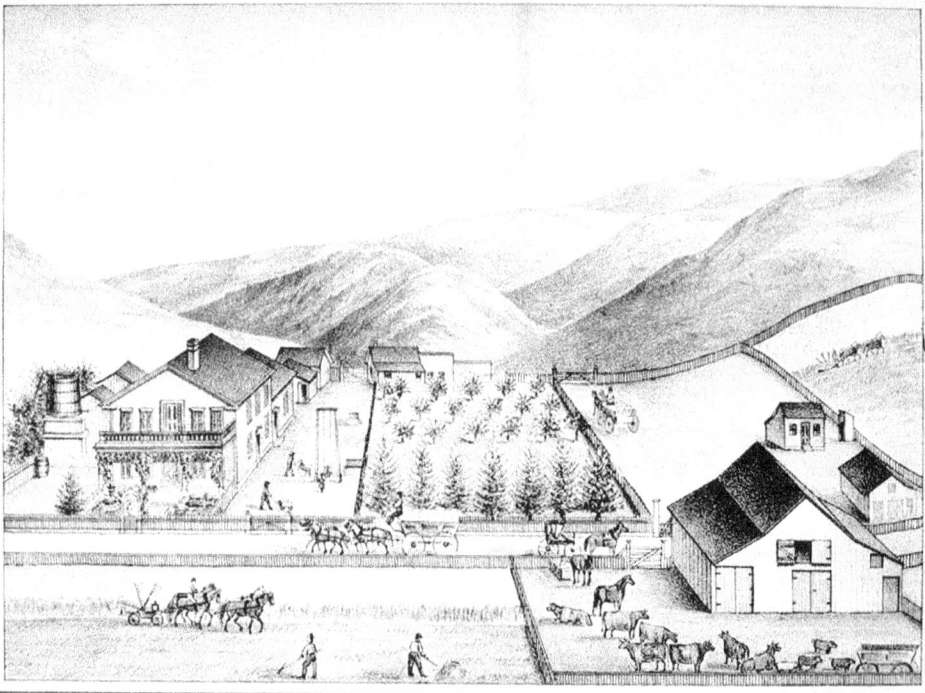

RESIDENCE & RANCH OF JOHN BUTT.

This farming operation in Purisima was run by John Butt and was across the road from the Dobbel farm. Today there is no trace of the cultivated fields, the building, or the barn as pictured in 1878.

Despite much destruction from an 1862 flood, the village continued to grow, serving farmers and loggers. There was even a brief oil boom in the 1860s. By 1900, when the redwoods had all been cut, the village went into decline. It was all but abandoned by the 1930s. This tombstone is one of the few reminders of Old Purisima.

Half Moon Bay became an important shipping center because it was blessed with the best natural harbor on the coastside near Pillar Point. During the Mexican era it was a full-fledged point of entry, and in 1867 Josiah P. Ames erected a wharf in what is today Miramar. Ames did much for the coastside in public affairs and was a prominent businessman and, later, warden at San Quentin. The wharf, about a quarter-mile in total length from the pier head, was located on the coast near the mouth of a small stream, "Arroyo de en Medio." Warehouses were built to store grain, baled hay, and potatoes for shipping to San Francisco. The Amesport wharf eventually proved to be neither protected enough nor large enough to serve as a port, and it became a favorite fishing spot. After years of neglect, the wharf disappeared. Today its only lingering reminder is a street name.

This c. 1918 photo shows an early motorcycle race on the sand by the Amesport wharf, which extended over the beach and into the water. In the background is the Palace Miramar Hotel and Cafe.

The Palace Miramar was designed by William Tolpke and constructed by Joseph Miguel in 1917. Dance bands entertained in the blue and gold ballroom. The palace was extremely popular during Prohibition and speakeasy days.

Adventuresome Portuguese from the Azores Islands came to the coastside in the mid-1800s when drought conditions made life difficult in their home islands. Some were experienced shore whalers, and they set up several whaling stations along the San Mateo County coast. One called Whaleman's Harbor was about a mile north of Pillar Point where the bluffs made an ideal lookout position. Whales were spotted swimming close to the shore, and an opening in the reef allowed the whaleboats to drag their dead quarry to the beach.

This section of a nautical chart shows how the configuration of the sea bottom made a natural channel for launching whaleboats and bringing in whales. When suitable prey had been spotted, two six-man (steersman, harpooner, and four oarsmen) whaleboats would quickly launch in pursuit. If they were successful, as they were about a third of the time, they dragged the whale from the sea and the blubber was cut into chunks that were then boiled down in large "trying" ovens to liberate the whale oil.

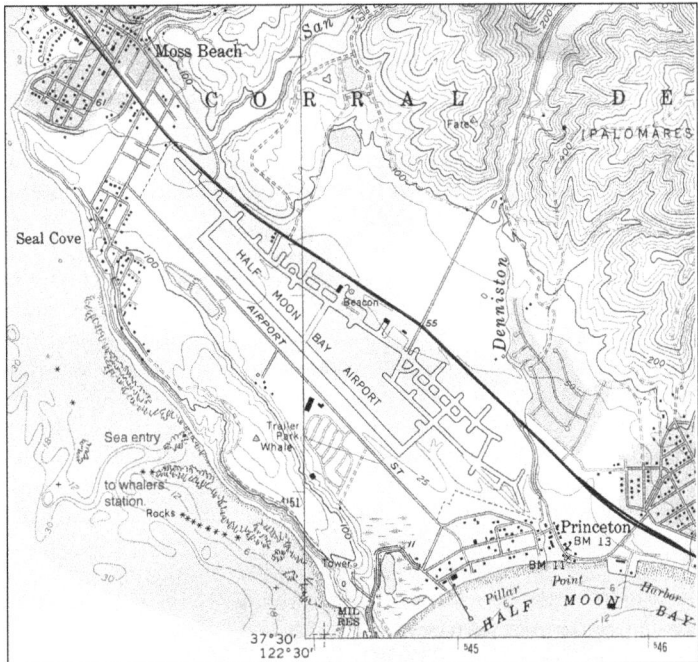

HARPER'S WEEKLY.

A JOURNAL OF CIVILIZATION

Vol. XXI.—No. 1069.]   NEW YORK, SATURDAY, JUNE 23, 1877.   [WITH A SUPPLEMENT. PRICE TEN CENTS.

Entered according to Act of Congress, in the Year 1877, by Harper & Brothers, in the Office of the Librarian of Congress, at Washington.

A WHALING STATION ON THE CALIFORNIA COAST.—DRAWN BY FRENZENY.—[SEE PAGE 485.]

This wood engraving by Paul Frenzeny, a famous American artist, appeared in *Harper's Weekly* in 1877. The whaling station pictured may well have been the one in Princeton. Whaling on the coast was described as such:

> Here and there along the coast of California may be found whaling stations, established chiefly by Portuguese or Sandwich Islanders. . . . Watch is carefully kept from an elevated lookout, and the raising of a flag is the signal to the fisherman on the beach that whales are in sight. The men instantly take to their boats and give chase to their prey. Harpoon guns and explosive bombs are used to dispatch the whale as soon as the boats get within striking distance, and the body is then secured and towed ashore, where the blubber is stripped off. It is tried out over ovens similar to those shown in the engraving, and the oil collected in casks for shipping. The whale most commonly taken in this manner is known as the "gray-back." A large one sometimes yields a profit of several hundred dollars.

The whaling industry became so intense and efficient that reductions in populations eventually made shore whaling unprofitable. Now that whaling is banned in most countries, whale populations are recovering.

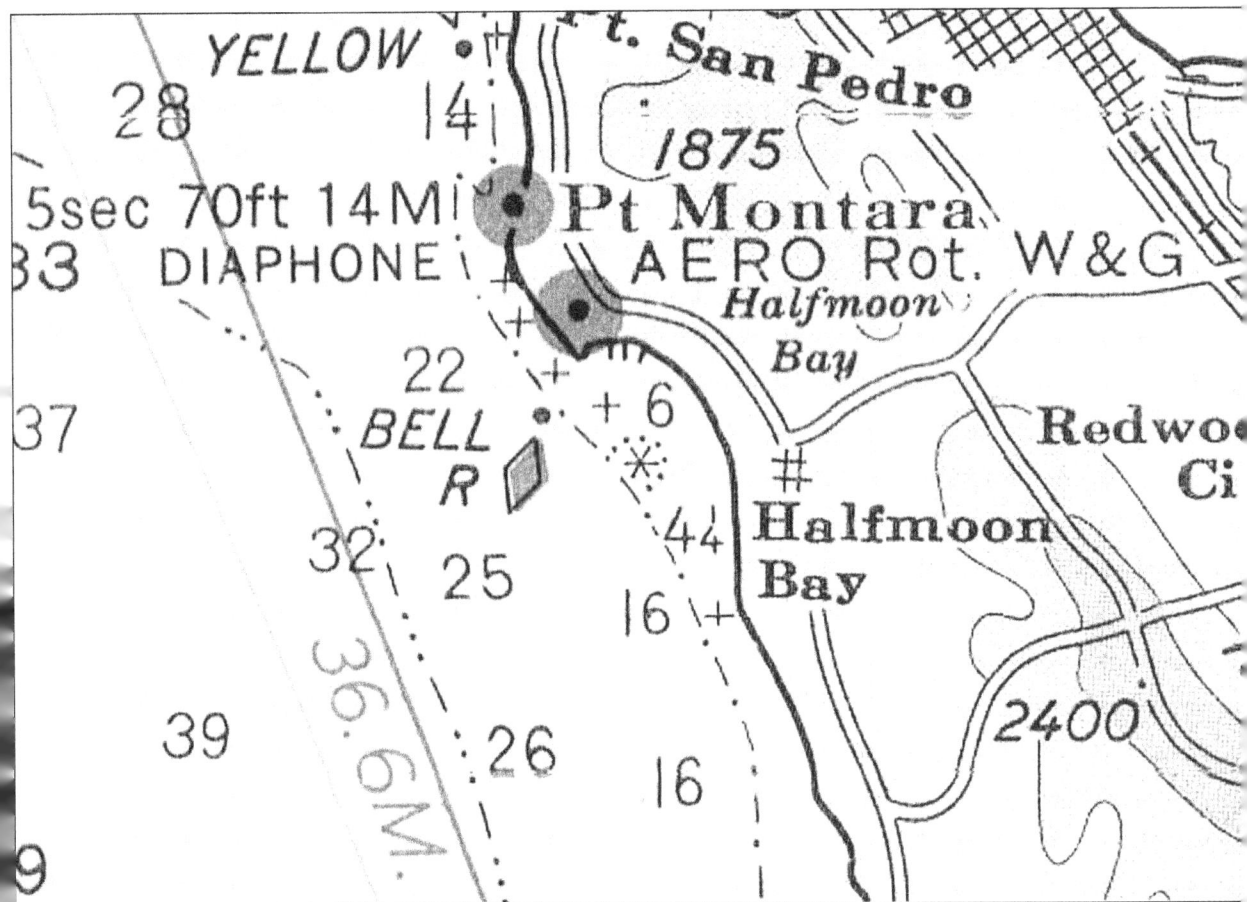

YELLOW
28   14
5sec 70ft 14Mi   Pt Montara
33   DIAPHONE   AERO Rot. W&G
                    Halfmoon
                    Bay
    22
37   *BELL*   + 6
      R   *
32   25   44   **Halfmoon**
                     Bay
              16 +
39   :26
          36.6M.
              16
t. San Pedro
1875

Redwo
Ci

2400

9

Each "+" on this chart shows the remains of a ship that came to grief in the Half Moon Bay area. For some of these wrecks, all remains have vanished:

Republic, sailing ship, ran onto rocks in a fog October 15, 1851.

Isabelita Hyme, clipper ship, carrying Chinese goods hit the rocks in a fog January 8, 1956.

Efina Kuyne, dutch galiot, wrecked on Pillar Point in January 1862.

Maggie Johnston, schooner, stranded at Half Moon Bay in 1863.

Mary Martin, schooner, stranded at Half Moon Bay in 1863.

Alert, schooner, stranded at Half Moon Bay November 28, 1868.

William Taber, steamship, hit the rocks in 1871.

San Ramon, steamship, ran ashore February 1, 1875.

Rydal Hall, sailing ship, carrying coal, wrecked on Pillar Point October 17, 1876.

Oceania, lumber schooner, sank off Pillar Point November 1896.

New York, sailing ship, beached in a gale March 13, 1898.

Leelanaw, steamship, ran onto reef September 23, 1899.

Californian, diesel ship, foundered off Half Moon Bay January 10, 1932.

Virginia, diesel ship, burned off Half Moon Bay October 14, 1932.

YP 636, U.S. Navy utility craft, went on the rocks in a fog September 12, 1946, carrying frozen tuna gathered at an atomic bomb test site to be analyzed.

The schooner *City of New York* was inbound from Hong Kong to San Francisco with a cargo of rice, tea, black pepper, jute, tapioca, and pineapples when it ran aground at Half Moon Bay Beach in heavy fog on March 13, 1898. The action of the surf caused the sand to all but swallow the wreck in only three days. Salvagers who bought the wreck for $5,000 operated quickly and were able to save cargo worth $25,000. (Courtesy of the San Benito Hotel collection.)

In 1875, Point Montara sounded its steam whistle to signal heavy fog. In 1900, an oil lantern and Fresnel lens was added. Even with the navigational aids, wrecks continued to occur in the area:
  Ada May (a.k.a. *Ida May*), two-masted schooner ran onto the rocks October 27, 1880.
  Alice Buck, sailing ship, carrying "railroad iron," ran ashore September 26, 1881. Eleven died.
  Argonaut, 105-foot schooner, ran aground November 4, 1890.
  Roma wrecked near Point Montara 1908.
  Grays Harbor wrecked near Point Montara 1922.
  Jugo Slavia, motorship, foundered 1928.

Map labels (left panel):
FORT POINT · FORT MASON · PRESIDIO SEE MAPS 36-137 · LOMBARD ST · GOLDEN GATE PARK 134-135 · ALMS HOUSE · HUNTER POINT · COLMA · CEMETERIES · VISITACION · EDGEMAR VBADEN · SOUTH SAN FRANCISCO · SALADA · BRIGHTON · SAN BRUNO · VALLEMAR · ROCKAWAY BEACH · SAN PEDRO · MILLBRAE · FARALLONE · MOSS BEACH · BURLINGAME · SAN MATEO · TO PESCADERO

FIREMAN'S FUND AUTOMOBILE INSURANCE COMPANY

SAN FRANCISCO TO

Map labels (right panel):
TO SAN FRANCISCO · SAN MATEO · GRANADA · BALBOA · BERESFORD · BELMONT · HALF MOON BAY · CRYSTAL SPRING LAKE · REDWOOD CITY · PURISIMA · WOODSIDE · LOBITAS · TUNITAS · SAN GREGORIO · BELLVALE · LA HONDA · PESCADERO · TO SANTA CRUZ

FIREMAN'S FUND AUTOMOBILE INSURANCE COMPANY

SAN MATEO — TO — PESCADERO VIA REDWOOD CITY 39.3 MILES

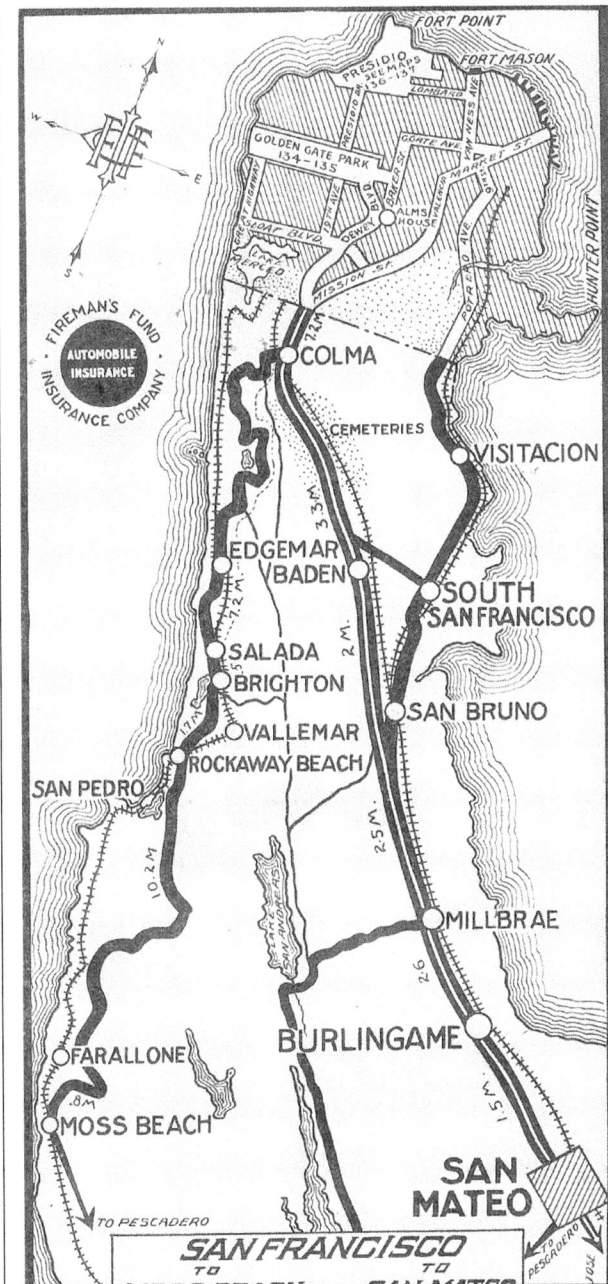

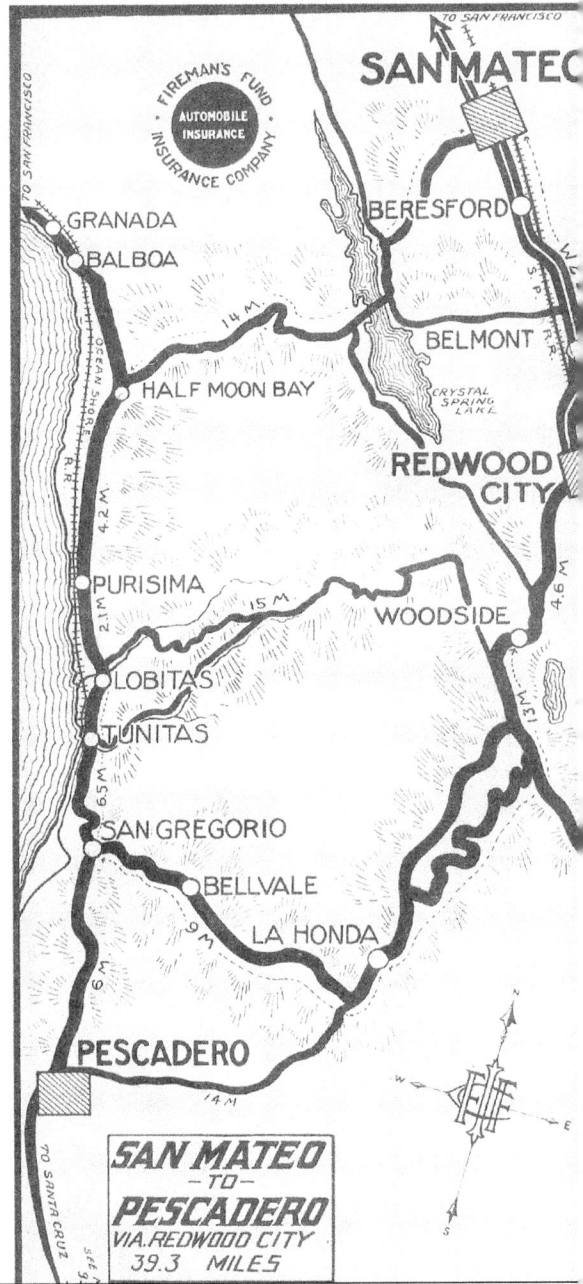

This 1916 road map shows the state roads leading to Half Moon Bay. Devil's Slide, part of San Pedro Mountain, was bypassed (see map) because of continuous slipping of the unstable mountain at the ocean's edge. The highway came to the coast behind present-day Montara, thereby avoiding Devil's Slide. However, the railroad tracks can be seen hugging the coast. These maps were produced by Fireman's Fund. They rated the roads as excellent, and noted they were paved and had garages and gasoline at all principal points. Today, Highway 1 follows the old coastal railroad route and provides one of the most spectacular views of the ocean far below. A controversial tunnel is now in the works to bypass Devil's Slide.

Montara. From this point a monument, erected on the spot from which the Bay of San Francisco was discovered in 1769 by Don Gaspar de Portola, is plainly seen. The road now leads towards the ocean and Montara Beach. Farallone is reached at 20.4; Moss Beach at 21.5; Marine View at 21.8.

Princeton Beach on the right. This particular beach is interesting because of a natural break-water or reef extending some two miles south. Because of this reef there is no under-tow on this beach. Granada and Ocean Shore station on the left. Straight ahead for Half Moon Bay. Miramar is passed at 25.6.

Road to the left leads to San Mateo (see page 7, picture 5). Go straight ahead for Half Moon Bay (see page 4, picture 1).

Half Moon Bay. Center of town. After a short run of 4.1, through a very fertile valley, Purisima is reached, a hamlet of pioneer days. The road as far as San Gregorio is under construction; will be completed about November 1, 1915.

For the 1915 Panama-Pacific International Exhibition, San Mateo County issued an illustrated pamphlet of automobile roads in the county (mileage is from the site of the PPIE in today's San Francisco Marina District) with the destination being Half Moon Bay on the coastal route. It was felt that many of the visitors to this great fair (held to show the world that San Francisco had totally recovered from the 1906 earthquake) would want to explore the adjacent San Mateo County areas and, hopefully, buy land and settle into one of the many charming coastside towns.

PUMPKIN FIELD, CALIFORNIA

Pumpkins became an important crop to the area. This 1940s picture shows a pumpkin field in Half Moon Bay. In the early 1970s an official festival was started with prizes for the world's largest pumpkin. The area itself produces about 3,500 tons of pumpkins every year. It is now a tradition for people from all over the Bay Area to select a Halloween pumpkin here. There are parades, pumpkin carving, and pie-eating contests.

Artichokes, Half Moon Bay, San Mateo County

Artichokes were perfect for the cool, foggy coastal growing area. The Italians brought this valuable cash crop to California. This picture from the 1920s shows a pretty spectacle of the growing plants. Northern coastal California production is only exceeded by Italy itself.

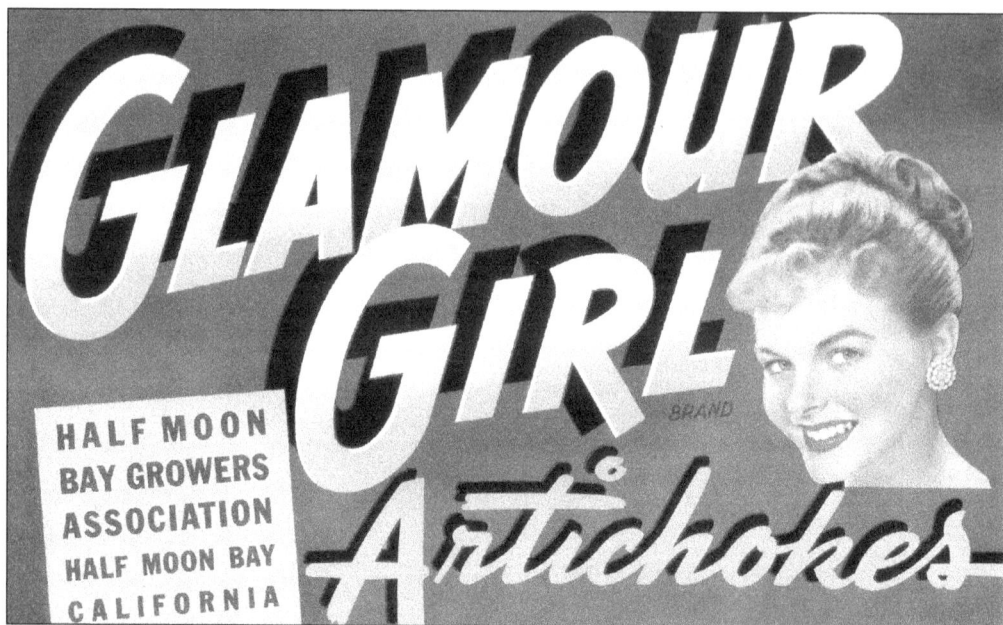

Around 1915, the Half Moon Bay Grower's Association was formed to promote the sale of artichokes, to help minimize marketing costs, and to promote their product. In the case of artichokes there was a learning curve, as most Americans were unfamiliar with the vegetable. Salesmen demonstrated the way to eat artichokes and how to prepare them. In his memoirs, Jack Debenidetti recalls how his father, John, gave up his business pursuits in banking and merchandising to become known as the "Artichoke King" by heading this association and traveling throughout the country promoting artichokes and demonstrating how to cook and eat them. Beautiful labels (often showing women) were designed, then lithographed and put on the sides of crates. Today, such labels are very collectible.

In its most neglected state, the James Johnston house was windowless and without part of its rear extension. In this photograph the ground around it was planted with Brussels sprouts. Like artichokes and cabbage, brussels sprouts are a crop particularly well suited to the soil and weather conditions along the San Mateo coast. Italian William Nerli, who had a farm that became the McNee Ranch, is credited with introducing this crop to the coastside.

Nurseries and farms began to line Highway 1 and Highway 92. Flower and nursery crops became increasingly important, eventually surpassing vegetables, dairy, and forest products. By 1999, the floral industry accounted for almost 80 percent of crop values. Above is a photo of Half Moon Bay Nursery in the early 1960s, when the area was hit by a very rare snowstorm.

At the coastside, transportation has always been a blessing or a curse, depending on one's point of view. Since the demise of stagecoach travel between San Mateo and the coast, the auto has reigned. Better roads were required. This 1920s postcard indicates the pride felt in the creation of the "Concrete Ribbon" Highway 92.

Highway 1 has always been bedeviled by Devil's Slide. Plans for a tunnel, over 50 years in the making, are about to be launched as a full-fledged project. This 1950s aerial view is dramatic evidence of the precarious situation of Highway 1.

Three

RAILROAD AND REAL ESTATE DEVELOPMENT

Real estate speculation, investment opportunities, recreation, and business sparked interest in the San Mateo coastside in the late 1800s and early 1900s. With the creation of Ocean Shore Railroad, it was anticipated the coastside would attract vacationers who would like the area so well that they would buy lands the railroad was given for its right of way. The existing farm population was attracted to the railroad because for the first time, produce could be shipped efficiently and quickly into the city. Farmers would no longer have to rely on the arduous journey by dray or boat.

Construction of the railroad began in 1905, and it was planned that the line would travel from Twelfth and Mission Streets in San Francisco over to the coast in what is today Daly City, and then south down the coast to Santa Cruz. The 1906 earthquake changed things. The damage was a terrible setback—costly in time and money. The original plan for a dual-track, all-electric locomotive system had to be scaled back to a single-track, steam locomotive system. However, by 1908 the line extended as far south as Tunitas. North from Santa Cruz it extended as far as Swanton. Jitneys between these two locations completed the trip. In anticipation of people swarming to the coast, many fancy resorts were planned in places like Montara and Moss Beach. A beautiful subdivision was planned for El Granada, with parks and boulevards lined with trees. The center of this hub of activity would be Half Moon Bay.

Real estate speculators and developers were important players in the concept and development of the railroad. Plans were made for a boom along the coast. They built 12 stations for the 14 miles between Montara and the former town of Purisima. Most of their dreams never materialized.

This *c.* 1910 photo shows that some stops were quite simple and consisted of little more than a platform.

ROUTE OF OCEAN SHORE RAILROAD

Line Will Open Rich Region Along Bay Shore Between This City and Santa Cruz.

WILL TAP COAST ALONG HALFMOON BAY VALLEY

Pescadero Valley, Wealthy in Agricultural Products, Will Also Be Opened Up by the Road—Will Make Fast Time

SANTA CRUZ, July 4.—With the active resistance now being offered the Ocean Shore Electric road by the Southern Pacific, the plans and route of the former are becoming subjects of great interest to the people on the line between San Francisco and Santa Cruz, which the road is to traverse. The main line of the Ocean Shore will begin in San Francisco at the China Basin, and proceed via Army and Kentucky streets, cutting across to the Coast line at Ocean View. Here a branch line to the Cliff House and the Presidio is to join the main line, which then heads for the Pedro valley, a rich and well-cultivated section. The Coast range between here and Halfmoon Bay is devoid of timber and cultivated to its highest points. The mountain range back of Halfmoon Bay, which is the next important point reached, is low and narrow and has a pass through which a branch line can be easily built to Alviso, at the head of navigation on San Francisco bay. Alviso is believed to also be an objective point of the Western Pacific. Halfmoon bay has

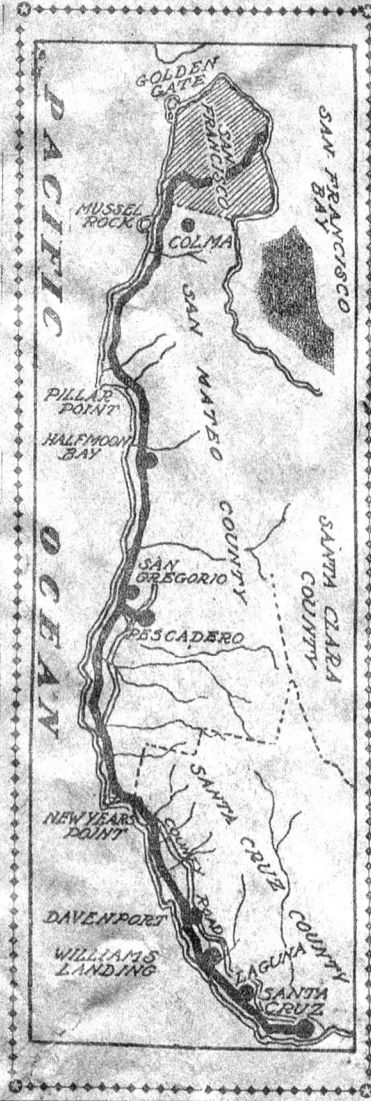

In 1905, the *San Francisco Chronicle* announced the following:

> . . . the line will open a rich region . . . will tap coast along Half Moon Bay Valley. The Coast Range between here and Half Moon Bay is devoid of timber and cultivated to its highest points. The mountain range back of Half Moon Bay is the next important point reached. Half Moon Bay now has two weekly newspapers, a bank, and a large number of businesses. It is already experiencing a boom as a result of this railroad plan; the land is fertile. There are large quantities of dairy and farm products. The population is about 2,000 people—largely increased on the prospect of rail transportation.

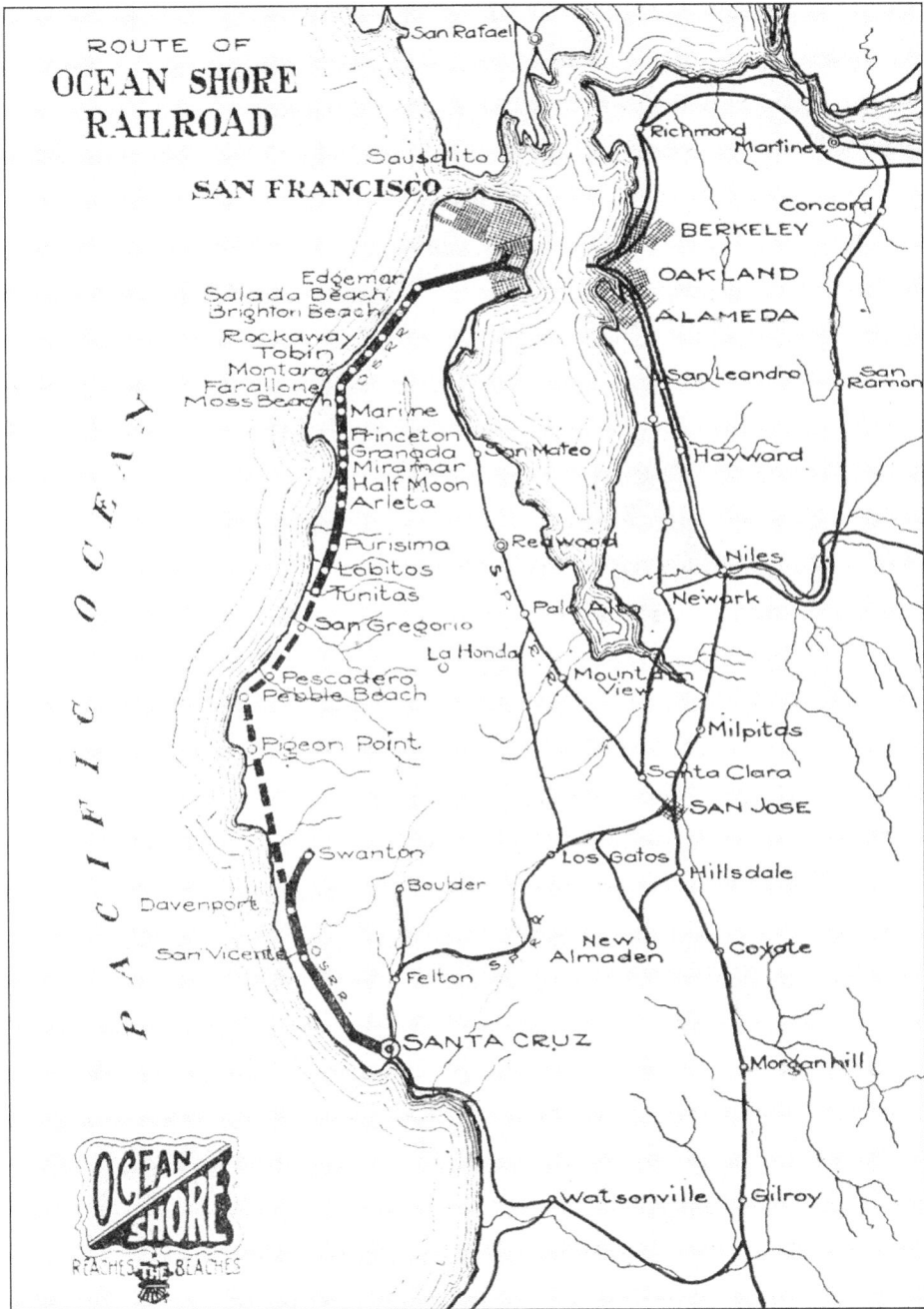

ROUTE OF
OCEAN SHORE RAILROAD

The Ocean Shore Railroad was intended to connect San Francisco and Santa Cruz over a dual-track, all-electric system. In addition to the 44 stations shown on this map, there was a rock-quarry loading chute at Ransom between Tobin and Green Valley. The chute straddled the tracks at the end of a south-end tunnel, on the perilous cliff side. The railroad was the first means of transportation to cross Devil's Slide. The Ohlones, early explorers, and residents took more circuitous inland routes over Montara Mountain. Recent CalTrans tests indicate that the unconsolidated sedimentary deposits that make the geology so unstable there extend around 1,500 feet into the face of the slope.

Two construction workers can be seen by the newly laid track. Although the route seems flat at this point, sections of the railroad were actually perilous cliffhangers.

A horse-drawn grader was essential in preparing the roadbed along the stretches of the Ocean Shore Railroad route that would not support the heavier mechanized equipment.

This is the old railroad station in Montara as it looks today. It is still on its original site on Second Street. The fieldstone walls are original, although the wood-framed section on the south end has been added. Montara is spelled out on the pavement.

This photo shows the railroad station in Farallone City. Sand was regularly hauled from the Keystone Company in Farallone to San Francisco.

A *c.* 1915 postcard view of the Railroad Station at Moss Beach shows no signs of development in the vicinity. A sign points to picnic and park areas, which were used to show off the assets of the area and encourage people to buy land.

The No. 22, a Baldwin Mogul, picks up a well-dressed crowd at the Moss Beach Station on a typical Sunday excursion *c.* 1915.

The railroad built their largest and most elaborate station at Granada to fit in with the layout of the community designed by Daniel Burnham.

GRANADA DEPOT
OCEAN SHORE RAILWAY

There were three stations in Granada, built one mile apart. The Old Granada station was utilized as a real estate office in 1935. (Courtesy of the Ted Wurm collection.)

This is a current picture of the former North Granada station, which was built in 1906. It has been modified and is now a restaurant.

This 1910 photo provides a rare view of the Half Moon Bay station. The passengers are very well dressed, as a train ride was a major event for most people. Note the old carriage to the right, on Kelly Avenue. (Courtesy of the Ted Wurm collection.)

In this *c.* 1915 photo, Locomotive No. 4 is shown stopping at the Half Moon Bay station.

54

The busy Kelly Avenue railroad station was moved after the Ocean Shore Railroad sold it when operations ceased in 1920. Later, it was moved again and became the social hall behind the Methodist Church at Miramontes Avenue. This September 1973 photo shows the old Kelly Avenue railroad station attached as an addition to the church.

When the church complex was expanded by new construction, the station was moved to its current location next to the James Johnston House, where it is used as a daycare center and for meetings of the Spanishtown Historical Society.

This is a *c.* 1915 photo of the Arleta Park station in Half Moon Bay, a wood-frame structure built in the vernacular railroad station style. The California Historic Resources Inventory Summary referred to the station as "uncharacteristically ornate for a small community depot."

The former Arleta Park station now serves as a private residence on Railroad Avenue. The external features have changed little from the original design, save for the enlargement and addition of a few windows. The home is near present-day Poplar and Railroad Streets.

Real estate companies encouraged growth along the railroad route. It was envisioned that people would flock to the coast and there would be a real estate boom. Postcards and newspaper ads were important tools to help sell lots.

Half Moon Bay Realty Company's prospectus shows its subdivisions dominating the peninsula. The company envisioned separate cities of Naples, Grand View Terrace, and Venice Beach.

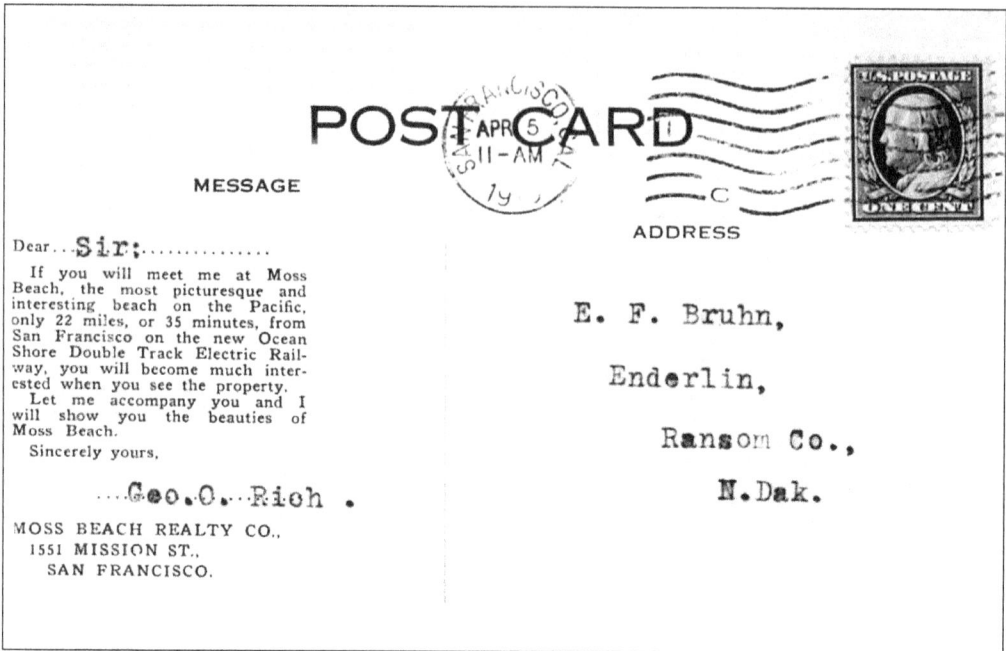

POST CARD

POST CARD

MESSAGE

ADDRESS

Dear...Sir:..............

If you will meet me at Moss
Beach, the most picturesque and
interesting beach on the Pacific,
only 22 miles, or 35 minutes, from
San Francisco on the new Ocean
Shore Double Track Electric Railway, you will become much interested when you see the property.

Let me accompany you and I
will show you the beauties of
Moss Beach.

Sincerely yours,

...Geo.O. Rich .

MOSS BEACH REALTY CO.,
1551 MISSION ST.,
SAN FRANCISCO.

E. F. Bruhn,

Enderlin,

Ransom Co.,

N. Dak.

This 1909 ad invites prospects to Moss Beach: "The most picturesque and interesting beach on the Pacific. . . . 35 minutes from San Francisco on the new Ocean Shore Double Track Electric Railway . . . " This postcard is addressed to a "prospect" in North Dakota—perhaps to even entice to buy "sight unseen."

A huge subdivision was planned for Farallone City that would have included all of today's Montara. This advertising postcard shows the route of the Ocean Shore Railroad. The cliffs of Devil's Slide can be seen just beyond Gray Whale Cove Beach in today's Montara, which is still an unincorporated area.

A swank, oceanfront hotel was envisioned for Moss Beach. The railroad station is seen in the rear right with a train approaching.

This is the front elevation for the proposed hotel. The arches and entrance way reflect a Spanish influence. These postcards are our only reminders of what might have been.

Granada

GRANADA—the magnificent Burnham City which will be to San Francisco what Atlantic City is to Philadelphia—what Coney Island is to New York —what Long Beach is to Los Angeles.

Within fifty minutes of San Francisco there is springing into life and activity a great and wonderful beach city—a place of amusement and pleasure for our growing city's 500,000 people.

San Francisco has waited patiently for Granada—waited until the courageous builders of the Ocean Shore Railway could overcome the great difficulties of construction necessary to gain access to the most remarkable stretch of clean, sandy, safe beach in the world.

Granada is now ready and welcomes you—invites you to spend Sunday on its broad stretch of hard sand, where the salty surf, tamed and calmed by a mighty natural reef, gently breaks and plays with the bathers along the shore.

The Spring opening of Granada takes place next Sunday—thousands will be there to enjoy the pleasures of that great event—to take advantage of the splendid opportunity to make large profits in Granada real estate, for now is the beginning, and every day of growth is adding dollars to the value of this magnificent property.

Come with us Sunday—enjoy a basket lunch on the Beach at our expense—let us help you to have the most enjoyable day of your life—get into the spirit of Spring— shake off the tedious grind of the daily commonplace—be happy next Sunday at Granada.

Special Trains leave Ocean Shore Depot, Twelfth and Mission streets, at 9:00 a. m., 10:10 a. m., 11:20 a. m., Sunday, May 2nd, 1909.

CHAS. H. KENDRICK CO.,
1284 Market St., San Francisco. Tel. Market 2854.
Dear Sirs: I am interested in Granada. Please send me tickets, so that I may visit this beautiful beach city.
Name ....
Street No. ....
City ....

For free tickets and particulars write or call on

Chas. H. Kendrick Co., Sole Agent

1284 Market Street, San Francisco   Telephone Market 2854

Branch Offices: Berkeley, Stockton, Fresno, Chico, Marysville, Sacramento, Vallejo

Advertisements touted El Granada as the Coney Island of the West Coast. Shore Line Investments built Granada's infrastructure. Thousands of trees were planted on hillsides (though promotional materials claimed hundreds of thousands of trees). Lots sold from $250 to $600. Renowned architect Daniel Burnham's plan called for curved, tree-lined streets, and beachfront amusements and parks were planned. Though curbs and concrete sidewalks were put in by 1907, San Francisco's quick recovery from the earthquake helped to stall the boom.

This real estate company proclaimed that Half Moon Bay was the "Coney Island of the Pacific Coast." The ad guaranteed sewer and water pipes laid by the seller for free. Free excursions were offered on the Ocean Shore Railroad.

This *c.* 1910 postcard shows the Riviera Tract located near Moss Beach.

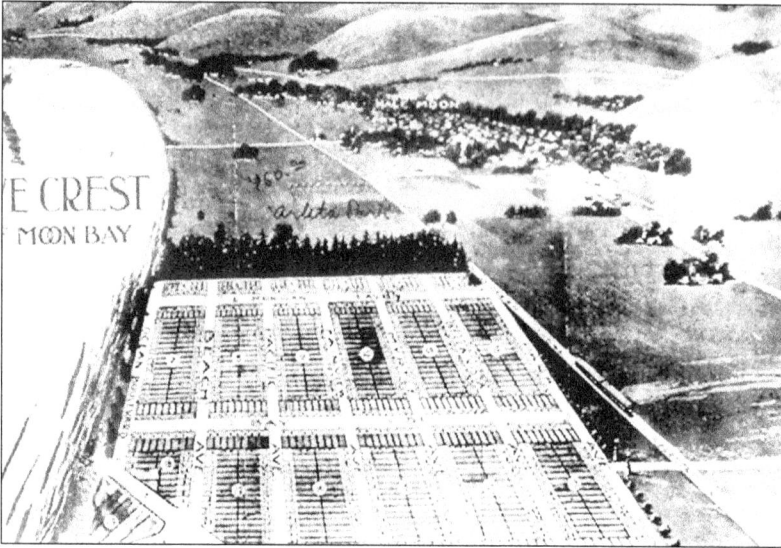

A large subdivision called Wavecrest was planned adjacent to the Arleta Park area. A total of 550 lots were sold for $220,000; however, very few of these original owners ever built on the lots.

The Ocean Shore Railway commissioned this reinforced concrete house to be built as a model in the Arleta Park subdivision. Paul H. Bosworth designed the Mission Revival cottage. This is how it looks today—on Poplar Street—still faithful to the original design.

The train was not just a business. Coastside artist and historian Galen Wolf described a typical Sunday excursion:

San Francisco was a town of many nationalities. Many of its people were recently from the "old country" and still retained the old ways. They formed singing, dancing, and musical groups, Turnvereins and Shutzen Vereins. And they dearly valued their social picnics. The Ocean Shore Railroad played up to this need. They ran picnic trains, open flat cars with benches, heaven bless their optimism as regards weather. These cars were filled on Sundays to capacity. The Italians, the Germans, the Hungarians, the French, the Irish and the Scots rallied to the depot in compact bands. They had their baskets, their wives, children, dogs, and above all, their music. At stations they favored the nations dismounted en masse and marched to the beaches. Here was a glorious romp for all. In the sun or in fog, the smoke of beach fires rose, and the sound of music playing made contentment tangible. It was a fine start for the day. But grandeur and the glory was in the return. In the dying light of the day, the fuming engine dragged its long train from beach to beach. And from the beaches the social and fraternal societies came marching. The day had put them in a splendid mood. There were proud, happy, cohesive and musical. At Princeton, the Italians came up to the station, accordions swinging and songs Venetian and Neapolitan. At Moss Beach mayhap, the Austrians or Hungarians with fiddles swinging, arms waving and seaside flowers in their hats. And then mayhap, though the dark and the west mist, the train bore its tuneful cargo, now tired and content, to their homes in the city.

With improved roads the automobile proved too popular. Railroad passenger revenues declined and the train ceased operation in 1920. Its legacy was the many towns and settlements that continued to grow and prosper long after the railroad's demise.

Railroads Cannot Be Run Without Patronage

Editor the Chronicle— Sir: 'Tis to laugh—the grief of the artichokers over the demise of the Ocean Shore. For years they shipped their stuff by truck—incidentally wrecking the highway—and stage lines are permitted to grow up and absorb revenue rightly belonging to the railroad. The Ocean Shore people have been rather good sports to have carried their enormous losses as long as they have in the face of the non-support of the villagers. There is no question but that their losses could have been materially decreased by the operation of lighter equipment in place of their heavy trains. One-man cars would have sufficed for most of the traffic. Now we have the picture complete: rusting rails, ruined roads, weeping wops and the grins of the gasoline barons.   S. O. LONG.

The last train ran on August 16, 1920. This letter to the editor of the *Chronicle* sums up the reason for the decline of the railroad. (Courtesy of the Ted Wurm collection.)

Four

WORLD WAR II
AND AFTER

World War II initiated another wave of change along the central county coast. On December 8, 1941, the day after the Japanese attack on Pearl Harbor, martial law was imposed along the west coast of the United States. Citizens of the Axis powers (Germany, Japan, and Italy) were forbidden to enter within a mile of the shoreline, preventing some from getting to their businesses. Fishing from boats was temporarily prohibited. The authorities fully activated and expanded the San Francisco Bay coastal defense system, built an anti-aircraft gunnery school at Montara, constructed a small airfield north of Princeton, and established round-the-clock Coast Guard beach patrols. The restrictions were soon eased to permit fishing from boats in the vicinity of their homeports. The scarcity of fuel reduced the range of all fishermen, including the bigger boats from San Francisco, and gave an advantage to the coastside boats.

The threat of invasion may have been exaggerated, but there was danger along the coast. In 1942, a Japanese submarine and a Standard Oil tanker exchanged gunfire off Half Moon Bay. Usually, the Japanese submarines got away after lobbing a few shells at coastside targets, but J125 was accidentally struck and sunk by a garbage scow near the Farallone Islands. After the war, many of the hastily built facilities were dismantled, and a new period began.

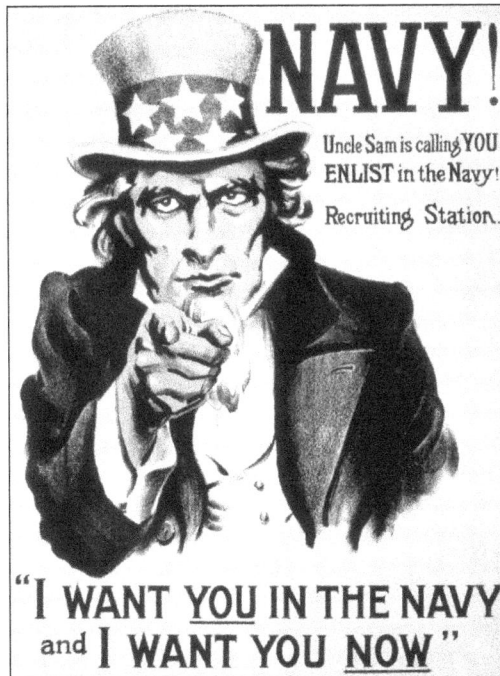

This recruiting poster was typical of the war years.

A system of 37 coastal defense guns protected the San Francisco Bay entrance from hostile forces. Numerous observation bunkers along the coast provided sighting data for the guns. This observation post, north of Montara State Beach, controlled 10 batteries of guns and included a power plant. The observation post was originally covered by the hill. Later, a Texan, Frederick Wagner, bought the site and began excavating a level house lot. He abandoned the project when he was unable to get the necessary permits.

Other elements included in the coastal defense of the area were a gunnery school and a battery of searchlights at Montara, four mobile 155-millimeter guns near Princeton, radar and searchlights at Pillar Point, and several data point markers like this one, located on the tidal flats below the Moss Beach Distillery. The data point at Purisima was the southernmost element in the system.

These barracks housed personnel at the anti-aircraft gunnery school established in Montara and consisted of about 40 semi-permanent buildings. As many as 3,000 personnel lived there during the peak of training activities, including 140 officers. Firing at target sleeves towed by aircraft from the newly built airfield north of Half Moon Bay, the trainees became familiar with the characteristics of 50-caliber machine guns and 40-millimeter anti-aircraft guns, then went on to their coastal defense duties. The Montara base was "disestablished" in May 1946.

A complex of bunkers near Point Montara Light Station protected numerous elements of the coastal defense system. Functional components at Montara consisted of a pair of 60-inch, 8-million-candlepower searchlights and a data point, in addition to the anti-aircraft gunnery school. Training at the gunnery school covered 50-caliber and 20-millimeter machine guns, and 40-millimeter and 3-inch rapid-fire guns.

The cluster of coastal defense system bunkers near the Little League field in Wavecrest includes this one (probably for ammunition storage), a similar one, and a smaller one that reportedly served as the pharmacy for troops in the area.

The U.S. Coast Guard patrolled the beaches during World War II to detect any enemy or subversive activity. Working from posts at Fort Funston, the McCloskey castle in Pacifica, this three-story house on the corner of Main Street and Kelly Avenue in Half Moon Bay, and a large home at Pigeon Point, the Station H men kept the beaches under surveillance on foot and on horseback 24 hours a day for the duration.

Station H included this Half Moon Bay corral and barn at 625 Purisima Street from which mounted guards patrolled the nearby shoreline. This photograph was taken from the third floor of the house in the previous picture (where La Piazza now stands). Specially trained dogs such as German shepherds "Buddy" and "Chuck" helped with the duty.

Seen here patrolling the Half Moon Bay shoreline are "cowboy sailors" (as the group called themselves) Daniel Orullian from Salt Lake City, Utah, and Ernest Lefebvre from Tacoma, Washington. This and the preceding two photographs are from the booklet *Station "H"—Coast Guard Beach Patrol, 12th Naval District.*

The government needed an airfield for Navy PBY patrol planes and for Army planes that would tow the target sleeves as part of the Montara Anti-Aircraft Gunnery School training. CalTrans created what is now the Half Moon Bay Airport just north of Princeton in 1943. It was transferred to San Mateo County in 1950 and now serves general aviation aircraft weighing up to 12,500 pounds. (Photo by Lloyd Easterby.)

Construction of the outer breakwater in 1957 blocked the normal gradual flow of sand southward along this section of El Granada Beach just south of the breakwater. Loss of the protective sand caused wave erosion and threatened to undermine Highway 1 until installation of a seawall of boulders stabilized the shoreline. (Photo by Lloyd Easterby.)

After the end of World War II, the Pillar Point installation evolved into an Air Force missile tracking station. Still active, it is operated under contract by the Grumman Corporation.

To young and old, Half Moon Bay and the word "beach" are interchangeable. These visitors, in their 1922 Overland Tourer, have stopped to enjoy the view. A sunny day brings thousands of people out to enjoy the magnificent sweep of sand that starts at the south end of the breakwater in El Granada and runs to Miramontes Point. The section of El Granada Beach just south of the breakwater, commonly referred to as "Surfers' Beach," has become a popular surfing spot although it has been necessary to build a seawall along that section to protect Highway 1 from being undercut by the waves. This photograph hangs in the San Benito Hotel.

In 1964, master builder Henry Doelger announced plans for a community of 50,000 on the land north of Half Moon Bay and east of the airport with a supporting landfill facility in Green Canyon south of Devil's Slide. He did manage to construct 220 houses at Clipper Ridge, north of El Granada, before the rise of environmentalism in the 1970s curtailed the plans. Recently, that land plus additional open space east of Moss Beach and Montara—over 4,000 acres in all of what is still called Corral de Tierra—is in the process of a controversial transfer to the Golden Gate National Recreation Area.

A traveler coming up the coast today sees the Ritz Carlton across the fields north of Purisima Creek. The new addition to the coastal resort scene on Miramontes Point has 261 rooms and two 18-hole golf courses. In the distance is the radar missile tracking station on Pillar Point.

Five

NEIGHBORING
COMMUNITIES

The communities north of Half Moon Bay developed into unique and interesting places. Given a boost or a beginning by the Ocean Shore Railroad, their growth slowed as the railroad declined. These areas of Montara (includes Farallone City), Moss Beach, El Granada, and Princeton remain today as unincorporated towns under the province of San Mateo County. They have all experienced slow but steady growth. The relatively inaccessible coast with its isolated beach coves, deserted roads, and foggy weather was a natural location for rum-running and bootlegging during Prohibition. Rum-running led to blind pigs (illegal drinking establishments) and bawdy behavior. The coast gained a reputation as a good place to go for fun and excitement. After Prohibition, many of these roadhouses and hotels lived on as respectable establishments. Coastal growth and development has been mightily affected by the 1972 Coastal Initiative. This act placed stringent conditions on development.

This c. 1915 Moss Beach photograph shows some early tourists on an arch formation that has since been destroyed by waves.

In land grant days and before the advent of the Ocean Shore Railroad, Montara was bucolic. The above 1878 lithograph from the *Illustrated History of San Mateo County* shows the ranch and dairy of Vic Guerrero, son of the original land grant holder. It was located in present-day Montara.

Montara's natural setting is one of beauty. Montara Beach is a pristine stretch between two high bluffs. As to how the community received its name, *Gudde's Place Names of California* states that "Montoro" was used by the Whitney Survey in 1867. The current spelling was introduced in 1869 by the Coast Survey. Gudde believes that both are misspellings of Spanish words referring to forests, mountains (a "Canada Montosa"), and valleys full of woods and thickets. Today, the word *montara* is used as the name of a town, a peak, and a point.

Harr Wagner, a San Francisco publisher and writer and a friend to most of the area's bohemian intelligentsia, founded an art colony *c.* 1908 in Montara. He envisioned an arts and crafts college surrounded by cozy self-sufficient cottages with stone fireplaces. He offered 400 lots at $150 each. Easy installments were arranged at $1.50 per week. As the Ocean Shore Railroad declined, so did the dream.

This early *c.* 1910 overview of Montara looks west toward the coast, Devil's Slide, and the McNee Ranch. The prominent building on the right with the turrets is the old town hall, post office, and general store. It was designed by Will Sparks and built in 1908 by Lawrence J. Kent.

This is a c. 1910 view of the lighthouse at Montara. Fog and wind can both create peril for the sailor. In 1873, Congress appropriated $15,000 for this steam-powered fog signal. The lighthouse itself was built in 1887. In foggy years it operated over 1,500 hours. The whistle was so powerful it was said to be heard in San Francisco. Since 1970, it has been an automated horn buoy. Today, the Point Montara Lighthouse Hostel is located here.

This is a present-day view of George Street's old town hall and post office, which have a new life as the Goose and Turrets Bed and Breakfast.

The Farallone Hotel was built in 1906 as a Victorian roadhouse near the railroad station. It has been altered greatly over the years, and became the Farallone Inn in the 1950s. Hints of the past can be found in Germman-themed, stained glass windows that date back to the original owners, and some old, red brick in the garden.

In 1939, the old railroad station at Farallone was still standing. Farallone gradually merged into the town of Montara. (Courtesy of the Ted Wurm collection.)

The old Montara Grammar School was built in 1915 and remained a grammar school until 1950. It was the Fuller family home until 1972. Its next life was as a hang-glider factory and living space. In the 1980s, it became a historical site and now houses the Hayward Dance Studio.

In this mid-1950s aerial view by Lloyd Easterby, Montara has grown but still retains its small-town atmosphere. Note the trees planted by Harr Wagner.

Juergen Wienke left Germany in 1881. Arriving at the coast, he envisioned its rosy future as a resort. He named the area Moss Beach for its notably abundant growth of sea moss, an edible seaweed.

This road, called "Wienke Way," leads to the site of the Moss Beach Hotel built by Wienke. The hotel burned in 1911 and was not rebuilt. Wienke remained prominent in Moss Beach business and politics.

These happy bathers in this c. 1918 postcard enjoy a day on the rocky coast in San Francisco's seaside suburb. They are described as gathering sea moss on the aptly named Moss Beach.

This postcard shows happy bathers enjoying "Midwinter Sport at Moss Beach, Cal. San Francisco's Seaside Suburb."

This is a *c.* 1915 view of the northern end of the bathing beach at Moss Beach.

This *c.* 1915 postcard is entitled "A Grove at Moss Beach." The cypress trees were planted by Juergen Wienke.

This popular restaurant, built by Charles Nye before World War I, was located facing the tidal pools and was positioned right over the sand. It was the coastside's first casino.

A popular speakeasy during Prohibition, The Reefs hosted such luminaries as Jack London and Luther Burbank. The location made it easy to bring in liquor, and its isolation helped to protect it from law enforcement.

Owner Charles Nye claimed he could get a day's supply of abalone right on the beach. Perched right above the surf, The Reefs was extremely picturesque during moderate weather. However, the setting was its undoing when it was destroyed by waves during a 1931 storm. It was rebuilt as Reef II, above the beach and back from the cliffs.

Prohibition was big business along the San Mateo Coast. "Land sharks" picked up the booze off the beach for local roadhouses but primarily for San Francisco. Mother ships stayed outside the 12-mile limit loaded with 35,000–40,000 cases of Canadian liquor. This photograph was taken at low tide at Seal Cove and shows the narrowness of the entrance. Imagine the difficulty of running through the breakers in the dark to land the whiskey.

Seal Cove in Moss Beach was a great place to land booze during Prohibition, as it was secluded. Luckily, a roadhouse had been built in 1917 on the bluff above. In 1927, it was known as Frank's Place when Frank Torres owned and ran it. All sorts of people rubbed shoulders at this successful speakeasy. After Prohibition, it continued as the Beach Hotel and Restaurant. This plate is an original piece of crockery from 1950s "Frank Torres Beach Hotel."

This restaurant, today known as the Moss Beach Distillery, is noted for its ocean view and colorful past. It has also inherited a ghost known as "The Lady in Blue." It seems that in the 1930s, a married lady who always dressed in blue was having an affair with the piano player when she died mysteriously. People swear they have seen her searching the premises for her lover. This modern photo shows Seal Cove on the left, the popular bootlegging site.

Dr. Sol F. Light of UC Berkeley began collecting specimens in 1916 at Moss Beach. Biology students from Berkeley would study the tidal pools on field trips. They slept on the floor of The Reefs and took their meals there. In 1969, the three-mile area of tidal pools became known as the Fitzgerald Marine Reserve.

Much of the three miles of reefs between Moss Beach and Pillar Point are protected either within the Monterey Bay National Marine Sanctuary or the Fitzgerald Reserve. At low tide, seaweed, crabs, sponges, sea anemones, mollusks, starfish, and other marvels of nature can be observed. The reefs are also a popular sea bird feeding site.

An early 1920s photo shows some development of summer homes and businesses in Moss Beach. Note the artichoke field in the foreground, bordering Highway 1.

This 1957 aerial view by Lloyd Easterby shows that the layout of Moss Beach has not changed much—many of the trees are the original cypress planted by Wienke.

Daniel Burnham—renowned Chicago architect and city planner and the man who laid out the 1893 Columbian Exposition—designed the city of El Granada. The natural setting chosen was near but not directly on the shore. Burnham chose a radial Beaux Arts design because this was to be the showplace of the Ocean Shore Railroad. The town was laid out in grand avenues of concentric circles to match the curve of Half Moon Bay. The avenues were 150 to 200 feet in width, and hundreds of thousands of trees were planted. Curbs and concrete sidewalks were in place by 1907. The lots were sold from $250 to $600. Casinos, hotels, and bathing pavilions were all expected to line the coast. The official name of the city was Granada when it was registered in 1907 (changed from Balboa). The "El" was added by the postal service in 1909. Although the railroad went out of business, the town kept its charm. This aerial photo from the mid-1950s shows the essential layout unaltered but there is no Coney Island atmosphere as envisioned by the planners. El Granada remains the only complete Burnham town in the United States.

El Granada was designed to have open spaces and vistas; there were 640 acres of open space behind the town. The old photo looks back at the future town from the bathhouse. During the few years of the Ocean Shore Railroad's existence, 1,727 lots were sold for a total of $976,780.

SURF BATHING AT GRANADA

This 1908 photo shows a group of young girls enjoying the surf. The Amesport pier can be seen in the far distance.

This c. 1910 photo shows a group of well-dressed visitors to the El Granada surf (note the formal hats). A two-story mission-style hotel was built in 1904. It was the town's first commercial building with 20 guest rooms, which were available for $2 a day.

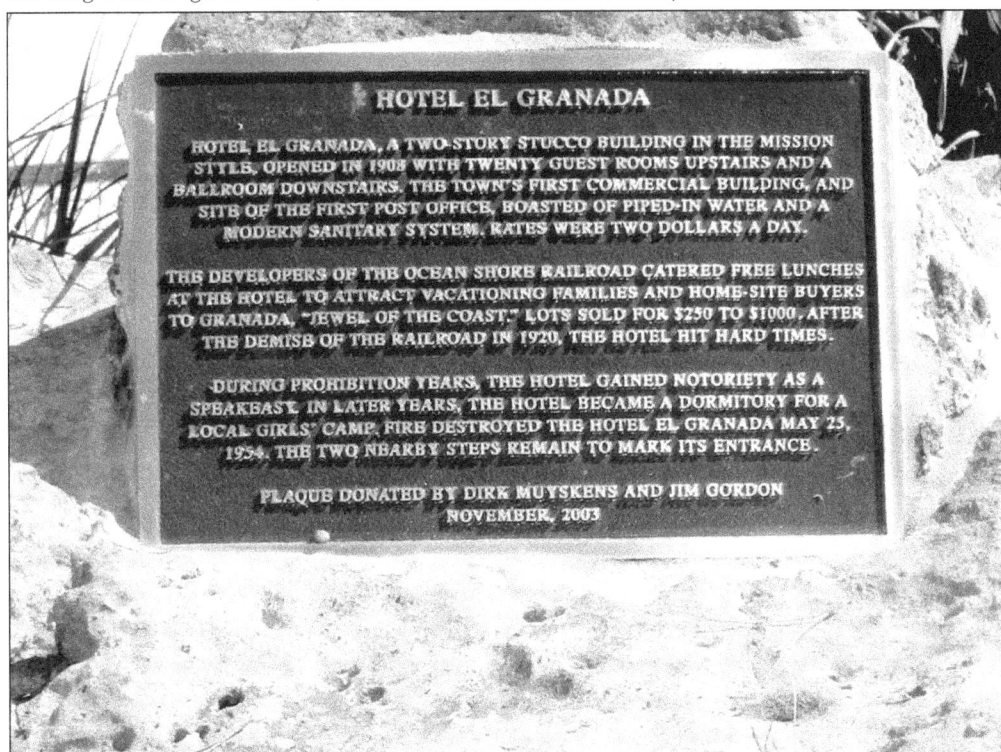

HOTEL EL GRANADA

HOTEL EL GRANADA, A TWO-STORY STUCCO BUILDING IN THE MISSION STYLE, OPENED IN 1908 WITH TWENTY GUEST ROOMS UPSTAIRS AND A BALLROOM DOWNSTAIRS. THE TOWN'S FIRST COMMERCIAL BUILDING, AND SITE OF THE FIRST POST OFFICE, BOASTED OF PIPED-IN WATER AND A MODERN SANITARY SYSTEM. RATES WERE TWO DOLLARS A DAY.

THE DEVELOPERS OF THE OCEAN SHORE RAILROAD CATERED FREE LUNCHES AT THE HOTEL TO ATTRACT VACATIONING FAMILIES AND HOME-SITE BUYERS TO GRANADA, "JEWEL OF THE COAST." LOTS SOLD FOR $250 TO $1000. AFTER THE DEMISE OF THE RAILROAD IN 1920, THE HOTEL HIT HARD TIMES.

DURING PROHIBITION YEARS, THE HOTEL GAINED NOTORIETY AS A SPEAKEASY. IN LATER YEARS, THE HOTEL BECAME A DORMITORY FOR A LOCAL GIRLS' CAMP. FIRE DESTROYED THE HOTEL EL GRANADA MAY 25, 1954. THE TWO NEARBY STEPS REMAIN TO MARK ITS ENTRANCE.

PLAQUE DONATED BY DIRK MUYSKENS AND JIM GORDON
NOVEMBER, 2003

A grand tourist hotel was built in El Granada during the railroad era. Unfortunately, it burned down in 1954, leaving only two steps as reminders. In today's El Granada, the most important links with the past are the original curbs and the wide boulevards.

This overview of the coastside's earliest seaport, Princeton, shows part of the fishing and yacht harbor. In the background the breakwater that protects Pillar Point and the harbor can be seen. Atop the point are radar installations.

This c. 1957 Lloyd Easterby photograph shows the building of the outer breakwater of Half Moon Bay harbor.

Princeton was developed in 1908 by Frank Brophy, who subdivided the area and sold 200 lots for $90,000 at Brophy's Beach and 225 lots for $123,700 at Princeton by the Sea. He named most of the streets after famous colleges.

The Denniston Creek Marsh is named after James Denniston, the first American farmer in the area, who in the 1850s planted grain on the flatter areas. The underlying aquifer is the only really productive well-water source along the San Mateo County coast.

Pictured is the Half Moon Beach Harbor looking past Capistrano Beach. It is remarkable because there are few harbors on the California coast. Commercial fishing vessels operate from here, catching salmon, halibut, and crab. Nearby restaurants and markets serve and sell fish and shellfish. There are 370 berths in the Pillar Point Harbor District. The number of fishing vessels has declined significantly in recent years. Sightseeing, whale watching, and sport fishing have increased.

Romeo Pier, the dock near the end of West Point Avenue in Princeton, was the fish-buying point until construction of the dock system started within the inner breakwater.

Built in 1908 as a resort, the Princeton Inn became one of the hot spots famous in the area during Prohibition. It figured frequently in the struggle between Prohibition agents to suppress the consumption of alcohol and the determination of a large segment of the population to continue to do so. In 1922, District Attorney Franklin Stuart attempted to close the inn under the provision of the Redlight Abatement Act. The Mezza Luna restaurant now occupies the venerable building at the corner of Capistrano Road and Prospect Way.

Hannah's Fish Trap in Princeton is a predecessor of today's Barbara's Fish Trap, a popular rustic fish restaurant. This is a watercolor by renowned local artist and historian Galen Wolf (1889–1976) who preserved much local history in oil, watercolor, and the written word.

The man in the photo is Jeff Clark, a world-renowned surfer at Mavericks off Pillar Point. In 1975 he became the first person to ever surf Mavericks. He continued to surf it solo for 15 years. Word finally began to spread and now Mavericks is at the forefront of modern, big-wave surfing, and attracts surfers from around the world. The challenging waves can crest over 50 feet. According to maverickssurf.com:

Mavericks breaks over an ocean reef that is one-half mile off the coast of Pillar Point . . . Until Jeff Clark took on the challenge of riding the wave, it was known only as a stretch of ocean to be avoided.

There is a deep water canyon to the west of Mavericks. The large ocean swells come from the north or west depending on the particulars of each storm, and move unobstructed through the deep water canyon west of Mavericks before being funneled towards the main bowl. . . .

When a significantly sized swell slams into the reef at Mavericks, it stops in its tracks and all that power gets launched out of the ocean like a volcano blowing its top . . . Mavericks, the wave that many believe to be the most challenging on the planet.

Six

YESTERDAY AND TODAY

Half Moon Bay has an amazing number of old houses and buildings that are still in use today. That such a variety exists is tribute to the skill of the architects and builders that worked in the area even before regularly passable roads had been built and to the preservation skills of those who have kept the buildings in good condition to form much of the charm that is Half Moon Bay today. Various writers have published descriptions of portions of this treasure. We have tried to compile a more comprehensive record of noteworthy structures and have corrected a few errors that in fact appeared in the previous material. We have added some new information obtained by interviewing local residents and have attempted to reconcile any discrepancies between information from the various sources. The collection of structures represents an interesting cross section of period architectural styles. The construction dates used are, in most cases, those that appear on the California Historic Resources Inventory sheets in the reference section of the Half Moon Bay Library. For ease of reference, the descriptions are listed by street alphabetically. For an excellent walking tour guide to many of the structures, get a copy of the Spanishtown Historical Society walking tour available at local bookstores. For the best set of photographs of old Half Moon Bay buildings available, get Kathryn Gualtieri's excellent but hard-to-find *Half Moon Bay—the Birth of a Coastside Town*.

This postcard shows the town of Half Moon bay as it looked c. 1910 from a slope to the east. Kelly Avenue runs up the middle of the photograph toward the ocean.

The Pilarcitos Creek Bridge replaced the old wooded wagon bridge in 1900. The commemorative plaque on the traffic side of the east railing (where it can only be read with difficulty or hazard) says, in part, "First Concrete Bridge/San Mateo County/J. Debenedetti, Supervisor" (in those days there were five district-elected county supervisors).

The 1885 house at 517 Church Street, with its gable facing the street, illustrates the expression of the Greek revival style that became known as the Pioneer style.

Across from the James Johnston House at 1800 Higgins Road is the Italianate T-plan house built by his brother William Johnston in 1854.

The John Francis House, built in 1930, is a Spanish Colonial revival–style home with an interesting variety of windows.

The Old Jail at 505 Johnston Street was built of reinforced concrete *c.* 1911 by private citizen John J. Higgins to be rented to the county—a common practice in those days. It was later acquired by the county and used as a sheriff's substation (an office and two cells) until about 1966. The county gave the building to the City of Half Moon Bay in 1989. It is now leased to the Spanishtown Historical Society.

Thomas Johnston built the barn behind the Old Jail in 1877 of random width vertical siding on a mudsill. It served the prospering fast freight business he had begun in 1867. It is now being converted into an agricultural museum.

In 1924, the Craftsman cottage at 601 Johnston Street was built as Dr. William A. Brooke's office.

The two-story Craftsman Bungalow–style house at 607 Johnston Street was built in 1913 for Joseph M. Francis, owner of Francis Brothers General Merchandise Store. He was a San Mateo county supervisor.

The Pioneer cottage at 611 Johnston Street was built in 1858 by James Johnston on a site to the west of his "White House" on Higgins Road. In 1865, it was moved to its current site. It was the first English-speaking school in the area. In 1872, it became Templars' Hall, part of the Temperance League that helped eventually bring about the Prohibition era.

The 1915 Craftsman Bungalow at 640 Johnston Street is distinguished by its oversized gable boards.

The cluster of Spanish Colonial revival buildings at 642 Johnston Street was built in 1920.

The 1900 vintage Queen Anne–style (note the turret) house was built for Ben Cunha. The columns supporting overhangs are evidence of Colonial revival influence. The house was later owned by the Alves family who had a dairy operation at the rear. It is currently the home of the Half Moon Bay Chamber of Commerce.

The current Our Lady of the Pillar Catholic Church faces Kelly Avenue on the corner of Church Street. A bell was installed in the first chapel of the same name in 1868. There is also a bronze plaque with the names of the original parishioners embedded in the sidewalk at the corner.

Still in use as a funeral parlor, the 1913 Zigzag Moderne–style commercial building at 645 Kelly Avenue has low relief ornamentation and sunrise motifs.

The California Vernacular/Pioneer two-story, shiplap-siding structure at 648 Kelly Avenue was built in 1900 as an annex to the Occidental Hotel and was connected to the hotel by a walkway.

The *Half Moon Bay Review* occupies the false-front Spanish Colonial revival building at 714 Kelly Avenue that was constructed in 1890.

The Simmons Home at 751 Kelly Avenue was built in 1865. Notable features are the wood shingle sheathing and the scalloped shingle bargeboard. The building is now in use by patent attorneys and is included on the National Register of Historic Places as No. 92000995.

Pablo Vasquez, son of Tiburcio and Alvira, ran the Pilarcitos Livery Stable with "rigs taken to and from hotel" service. The Greek revival–style "Priest's House" at 270 Main Street was built by Pablo Vasquez in 1869. Note the Tuscan pillars at the front door. The Vasquez family adobe was just to the west. Pablo Vasquez was noted for his horsemanship and billiards skill. This photograph hangs in the San Benito House.

Today, 270 Main Street serves as a real estate office, but most of the original architectural features are intact.

Built in 1930, the false-front–style business complex at 315 Main Street was known as the "Tin Palace" because of the corrugated iron sides and roof.

Spaniard Estanislao Zaballa built the house at 324 Main Street in 1859. The small front section may have been added later. Estanislao married Maria Dolores Miramontes, eldest daughter of Candelario Miramontes. This photograph of the family hangs in the lobby. For a time, Estanislao operated the San Benito General Merchandise Store and Saloon (before selling it to Debenedetti and Ceregnino in 1872) on the corner of Main and Mill Streets. He also had three stables in town.

Local resident Dave Cresson rehabilitated Zaballa House in 1979 as a bed and breakfast. The northeast corner rooftop quoin and decorative saw work are notable features that have been preserved. This is the oldest standing building in Half Moon Bay.

The Italianate commercial-style San Benito Hotel at 356 Main Street was built after the previous structure on that site, the Debenedetti and Ceregnino store and saloon, was razed due to heavy damage by the 1906 earthquake. The hotel was initially run by the Daneri family as the Hotel Mosconi. In 1915, it was sold to Frenchman Eugene Faus who renamed it Hotel Half Moon.

In the 1970s, Carol Mickelsen, Ron Mickelsen, and Dave Cresson rehabilitated this corner and established a bed and breakfast known as the San Benito House. The hotel originally had an open second-story balcony all around the Main Street and Mill Street sides; the balcony was removed to admit more light to the first-floor rooms. The building and its beautiful grounds are used for special occasions.

This 1920s photo shows the view south down Main Street from the Mill Street intersection. The buildings were, from left to right, (left side of the street) an auto service garage where the Half Moon Bay Inn now stands; 415–421 Main Street, still in use by three shops; 429 Main Street, which is now a lighting shop; 435 Main Street, substantially modified and now housing the Main Street Grill; and, barely visible beyond the parked cars, the Bank of Half Moon Bay, now the city hall; (right side of the street) the Oddfellows Hall (the taller of the two light-colored buildings in the distance) which is still in use; an unidentified building; the original Cunha's Country Store with its distinctive turret, rebuilt in 2004 after it burned down; two small unidentified buildings; and the Debenetti Block, which still stands at 400–416 Main Street.

At 400–416 Main Street is the J. Debenedetti Block, a Mission revival commercial complex built in 1906. It was the first reinforced concrete building in Half Moon Bay. After the Debenedetti and Ceregnino General Merchandise store on the northwest corner of Main and Mill Streets was so badly damaged in the 1906 earthquake that it had to be destroyed, Joseph Debenedetti rebuilt on this corner. The business nearest to the corner was the second location of the Bank of Half Moon Bay. The building is still in use.

The Pastime Club was an old-style saloon with the beautiful mahogany woodwork common in pre–World War II days. The San Benito House staff believes the Pastime Club was located in the middle of the Debenedetti Block. This photograph hangs in the San Benito House.

In 1922, 415–421 Main Street was built for Manuel Francis, the son of Portuguese settlers who became a San Mateo county supervisor. Living quarters were built over the shops.

In the 1880s, 429–431 Main Street was built for Angelo Boitano. It was occupied by Mateo Orsi's barbershop in the early 1900s.

The Spanish Colonial revival building at 433–435 Main Street was built in 1890. It once housed the Eagle's Nest Saloon, a bar owned by Toni Quinlan. Later it was the site of Red's Place, the restaurant and soda fountain run by Red Kerrick. Heavily altered, it is still in use.

To the left of the 1920s-era view to the north up Main Street from the Kelly Avenue intersection is the old Cuhna's Country Store, which was built around 1900 by Joseph Debenedetti as the Francis Brothers General Merchandise Store, and the Index Saloon run by Manuel "Sea Lion" Lewis.

The Cunha's Country Store was destroyed by fire in 2003. One of the last original general stores in the Bay Area, the local favorite was rebuilt with less ornamentation and was back in operation by 2004.

The Beaux Arts–style building at 501 Main Street was built for the Bank of Half Moon Bay in 1923. The property was formerly the site of Stephen (Esteban) Vidal's bakery for about 30 years before being converted to a dry goods store in 1892 and then to Mr. Snead's drug store in 1894. Vidal was born in Lerida, Spain, about 15 miles from the birthplace of Gaspar de Portolá. The older building was razed to make room for the bank. The bank was soon absorbed by the Bank of Italy, which became the Bank of America. Today, 501 Main Street is the Half Moon Bay City Hall.

The Half Moon Bakery was built in 1927 for Nat Castiglioni. It remains a bakery, and the original brick ovens are still in use.

Still "cookin' " after 77 years, these are the Half Moon Bay Bakery brick ovens.

In 1924, the Mission revival, commercial-style building at 521–523 Main Street was built for Tom and Mitch Picci. The curvilinear parapet, a Mission revival feature, is called an *espadana*.

The building at 522–526 Main Street, at the far left in this 19th-century photograph, was built in 1896 to replace the original hall that had burned in 1894. The Oddfellows have occupied it since 1900. Over the years, it has also housed the Native Sons of the Golden West, the Masons, and the Coastside Lutheran Church. (Courtesy of Jim Bell.)

Oddfellows Hall has been modified by the addition of the enclosed staircase on the left and by removal of much of the original ornamentation.

Once known as Angelo Boitano's General Merchandise Store and Saloon, the false-front Italianate building at 527 Main Street was built in 1873. Until the last reconstruction of the sidewalk a few years ago, the only remaining hitching post in the city stood in front.

Today, the building at 527 Main Street retains the early architectural details, although the entry and windows have been modernized.

The Colonial revival, classic-box building now housing a dentist's office at 538 Main Street was originally constructed for John W. Gilcrest in 1907 by the son of an early Irish immigrant.

This 1882 postcard looks north on Main Street from the Miramontes Street intersection. Pictured is the original hall predating the hall now occupied by the IOOF, two smaller buildings that are gone today, and the original Cunha's Country Store (on the left side of the street). On the right are a turreted building at 435 Main Street, Esteban Vidal's bakery (behind the front porch next door), and Angelo Boitano's General Merchandise Store and Saloon.

Carpenter and contractor Manuel J. Bernardo Jr. built this house in 1912.

Joseph W. Debenedetti, a businessman and San Mateo county supervisor, built this house at 711 Main Street in the 1870s. Once called the "artichoke king," Debenedetti is credited with introducing artichokes to consumers far and wide. The house originally sat at 416 Main Street, and its ground floor was used as the town's first post office. In 1906, Frank Bernardo bought it and relocated it to its present site by rolling it on logs.

The Mission Revival IDES Hall (Irmandade do Espiritu Santo, Portuguese for Brotherhood of the Holy Spirit) at 735 Main Street was built in 1928 to replace a 1911 wooden structure. IDES stages the Chamarita Festival each Pentecostal Sunday to commemorate the seemingly miraculous arrival of a food-laden ship in the Azores at a time when severe drought had brought the population to near starvation. The building also serves as headquarters for the annual Pumpkin Festival.

This Vernacular Pioneer–style house with Eastlake detailing was built in 1895 and is located at 775 Main Street. It features shiplap siding on the first story, fish-scale shingles on the second story, and dentils and stick ornamentation on the entry.

This Princess Anne–style (that is, Queen Anne without a turret) building at 779 Main Street, now the Old Thyme Inn, dates from 1898. Built by schoolteacher and principal George F. Gilcrest, it was purchased in 1904 by Alvin S. Hatch, son of pioneer lumberman Rufus H. Hatch.

This charming 1878 lithograph of the William Metzgar house (which was built in the 1870s at 940 Main Street) appeared in the *Illustrated History of San Mateo County*. This exceedingly rare book, published by Moore and DePue, depicted prominent businesses and homes.

This recent photograph of the old Metzgar house indicates that the Greek revival–style structure has been modified very little. The fanciful landscaping is gone and the wing at the right has been extended. It is now a private residence.

The Methodist Church at 777 Miramontes Avenue was designed by noted architect Charles Geddes and built in 1872. In Gothic revival–style, it features shiplap siding, a gable roof, lancet windows, and a Victorian octagonal belfry that permits a view of the bell from all angles. Although thrown from its foundation in the 1906 earthquake, the church was fully repaired within about a year. The building is included on the National Register of Historic Places as No. 80000854.

This group of buildings, including the Salt Box–style, Pioneer barn built in 1895, stands at 340 Purisima Street.

The Giannini house, also known as the "Sea Lion" Lewis house, is a false-front, Italianate house at 415 Purisima Street that was built in 1880.

The house at 546 Purisima Street is named for Ed Campbell, an early settler who built the Gothic revival structure in 1884.

Known as "the Borden Barn," this 1905 vintage vernacular western barn at 625 Purisima Street was used as a stable for U.S. Coast Guard beach patrol horses during World War II, then by Peterson Tractor Company. It was also known as the Westinghouse barn before being converted into an office building.

At 630 Purisima Street stands the Frank Bernardo house, a Queen Anne Craftsman Bungalow built in 1893.

The Queen Anne cottage at 505 San Benito Street, once known as the Ignace family house, was built in 1880.

The two-story structure at the rear of 505 San Benito Street was originally the Half Moon Bay Bakery.

The 1930 Mediterranean revival home at 523 San Benito Street sits in front of the site of the Edward Schubert's Half Moon Bay Brewery, which was in operation before 1890.

A number of other historically interesting houses exist along the highways leading out of Half Moon Bay. Heading east, this house in the group of buildings known as the Spanishtown Art Center was built in 1903 in the Period revival/Colonial revival style. Doric columns support the front porch.

Behind high shrubs, at 12011 San Mateo Road, is an 1885 Pioneer Vernacular–style house. Note the paneled bay, a common feature of coastside farmhouses.

The white Victorian house at 70 Pilarcitos Creek Road on the left beyond the Half Moon Bay Nursery was built in 1870 for the Albrecht family, immigrants from Germany who are buried in the old Catholic cemetery. The two-story, T-shaped Greek revival house later became known as the Pease House.

From Highway 1, this *c.* 1885 Pioneer Vernacular house can be seen at 38 Frenchman's Creek Road.

At 1820 North Cabrillo Highway, in the Friendly Acres/Sea Horse Ranch complex, is a *c.* 1864 Pioneer Vernacular house, with Gothic revival touches in the windows and doors.

The farm complex with the Pioneer Vernacular main house at 2711 Cabrillo Highway dates from 1870.

With a last look down 1920s Main Street past the Pilarcitos Creek Bridge, we can see several of the venerable buildings that help give Half Moon Bay so much of its charm.